LEARN
ZF2
zend framework 2

Learning
by Example

Slavey Karadzhov

ISBN-10: 1492372218
ISBN-13: 978-1492372219

FOREWORDS

"When we started Zend Framework we wanted to leverage the new sophisticated object oriented features of PHP 5 and take advantage of significant performance and security enhancements. That is what we achieved with Zend Framework 1. But our vision was to have a modular framework that can improve the reusability and allow easy integration of different existing modules into one application. Picking up a shopping cart module and dropping it into an application should be easy as a drag and drop operation. With Zend Framework 2 (ZF2) we achieved this and I am happy that you are holding in your hands the book that captured and explained all features of the most popular PHP framework that makes programming both art and pleasure. In this book Slavey shares his real life experience with ZF2 projects, as a senior consultant at Zend Technologies, and hits all the major challenges you may face. It is a must-have if you want a quick start and proficiency in ZF2. We wish you a pleasant reading."

Andi Gutmans & Zeev Suraski,
Founders of Zend Technologies

THANK YOU!

I would like to thank everyone in the Zend Framework team and community for their fantastic work during the years.

I would like to express my gratitude to the many people who helped me throughout the process of writing this book: to all those who provided support, talked things over, read, wrote, offered comments, allowed me to quote their remarks and assisted in the editing, proofreading and design. Special thanks go to my editor Doug Bierer and graphic designer Jivko Gradinarov for polishing this book. And to all early reviewers. You guys rock!

Above all I want to thank my wife, Tatiana and the rest of my family, who supported and encouraged me despite all the time it took me away from them.

TABLE OF CONTENTS

INTRODUCTION

Zend Framework 2 (ZF2) has changed the way to develop PHP applications and like every revolution takes time to be digested. ZF2 is quite new, released in September 2012, and it offers so many new features that the documentation available online is not fully comprehensive. For that reason I decided to write this book and try to show you what you can do with Zend Framework 2 (ZF2) and how to use its components as best as possible. The chapters in this book will lead you through the different components and in the process we will build a complete application. The recommendations in this book are based on my own experience as a programmer and Senior Consultant at Zend Technologies and reflect problems that our customers are often facing when using ZF2.

In contrast to other ZF2 books or sources of information that mention something can be done, but forgot to tell you why and how, this book tells you exactly how these things are possible and points out best practices and pitfalls of which you should be aware.

This book is for developers that are already skilled with PHP 5.3, can write object oriented code, and have mastered namespaces. Other developers are also welcome, but at times they may experience difficulty understanding solutions to problems presented in the book.

The chapters in the book are accompanied by source code that you could copy, and it will help you to learn by example.

Why Use Zend Framework 2

Zend Framework 2 is a PHP framework that helps you to develop applications faster, of various types, including web applications, web services and pure command line applications. It speeds your development through ready to use general components, saving you the need to write the code yourself and fostering reusability across multiple projects. And last but not least ZF2 is an actively developed framework backed by a huge community that is improving it every hour.

Let's list shortly some of the advantages:

Extensible

"Easy to adapt the framework to your needs"[1].

ZF2 allows you to use logically grouped parts of the framework, called components, without the need to use the complete framework. As an example, you might have an existing project which could benefit from existing ZF2 components such as Zend\Log without the need to completely restructure the existing legacy code. These components are flexible enough to allow adapting them to your own needs. Continuing with the example of Zend\Log - using it you can not only specify where you want to save the log messages (for example file, database or sending via email), but you also have the ability to determine which messages are of interest in the current application environment.

Modular

"Building blocks that can be used piece by piece with other applications or frameworks"

Reusing existing components is good, but not good enough. Instead of creating a user management block of code for every new application, why not reuse an existing one, or use an existing shopping cart implementation block? All that now can be done with ZF2. The good news is that it can be as simple as making the existing block a requirement for our current application and adding one line in the main configuration file to enable that block. The building blocks of the project are called modules and are discussed later in this book.

High Performance

"Engineered with performance tuning in mind"

PHP is an interpreted language, said to be quite fast as well as quite forgiving. ZF2 has fast autoloaders that allow your application to load only the PHP files that are required. Furthermore, the event based architecture ensures that only the code that is needed will be requested and executed. Thus the initial overhead is relatively low and the application's performance will be good even when its size and complexity grows. In this book I will provide you with hints that can speed up the application even more.

Secure

"All the cryptographic and secure coding tools you need to do things right"

Zend Framework 2 comes with a component called Zend\Crypt that will help you to deal with symmetric or asymmetric (public/private) algorithms and generate cryptographic fingerprints in order to protect and authenticate sensitive data. In addition, there is built-in security in the components that process incoming data from non-trusted sources. An example of this would be the processing of form data submitted from your visitors.

---

1 The quoted first sentence in the paragraph is taken from the ZF2 web site at the time of the writing of this book.

Community

"A vibrant and active contributor and user base for getting help and giving back"

Zend Framework 2 represents not only the work of full time Zend Technology employees, but also a community effort supported by a huge number of active contributors. This means that work to make the framework better is taking place even as you read this book. In October 2012 at the ZendCon conference, the lead developer of the framework, Matthew Weier O'Phinney, mentioned that the contributors are from 14 time zones[2] and they are literally improving it every single hour.

Enterprise Ready

"A proven history of success running business critical and high-usage applications"

"Enterprise ready" may sound like a marketing tag without any meaning, but in the case of ZF2 its meaning is that it:

- Has components that are proven to work
- Is built with security and performance in mind.
- Can be used in big projects and extended for your needs.
- Will save time and money bringing your product to the market

I have now briefly summarized the advantages of ZF2. We will see these advantages in action in the coming chapters. Let us now start developing our first ZF2 application.

---

2 http://www.youtube.com/watch?feature=player_detailpage&v=MAQvj_YeN5U#t=1014s

Installation

Requirements

Before we start the installation the following requirements must be met:

- You must be running PHP version 5.3.3 or later.
- You should use[3] a web server which supports URL rewriting. In this book we will use the apache web server with mod_rewrite predominantly. Zend Framework 2, however, can work on any web server that supports URL rewriting. Make sure that your apache server is configured to support .htaccess files.This can be achieved by changing the value of the directive **AllowOverride** to **FileInfo**.
- Use the Version Control System (VCS) **git**[4] to access the application source code that accompanies the chapters in the book.

Download the Skeleton Application

Use git and clone the skeleton application that comes with this book with the following command:

```
git clone https://github.com/slaff/learnzf2
```

Once git finishes cloning the repository you will have the latest version of the source code. It should be located in a folder called **learnzf2** in the current directory. Next we need to rewind the cloned repository to the beginning. To accomplish this you should execute the following command:

```
cd learnzf2/
git checkout 'ch-installation'
```

Now we need to fetch the ZendFramework 2 library.

Get Dependant Packages

With the help of **composer**[5] we will fetch the dependant packages for our application. In the beginning we need only the Zend Framework 2 library to start working. This can be accomplished by executing the following command from the application directory:

```
php composer.phar install
```

This command may take some time to finish. If it times out, you can try it again, but be sure to provide a specific environment parameter:

```
COMPOSER_PROCESS_TIMEOUT=5000 php composer.phar install
```

The version of composer.phar that comes with the skeleton application may be outdated. If you get error messages after running *composer.phar install* saying that the requested package 'zendframework/zendframework' could not be found then run the following command:

```
php composer.phar self-update
```

And execute again the *composer.phar install* command.

---

3 For pure development it is actually possible to skip this requirement because PHP version 5.4 has a built-in web server that can be used. We will demonstrate it later in the book.
4 http://git-scm.com/book/en/Getting-Started-Installing-Git
5 http://getcomposer.org

Setup

After downloading the skeleton application you can create a virtual host from which you can more easily access the web application. One example of a virtual host definition is given below:

```
<VirtualHost *:80>
    ServerName learnzf2.localhost
    DocumentRoot <full/path/to/>/learnzf2/public
    SetEnv APPLICATION_ENV "development"
    <Directory <full/path/to/>/learnzf2/public>
        DirectoryIndex index.php
        AllowOverride All
        Order allow,deny
        Allow from all
    </Directory>
</VirtualHost>
```

For development purposes, only if you have PHP 5.4[6], then you can just write

```
php -S 0.0.0.0:80 -t <full/path/to/>/learnzf2/public
```

Performance and Security Notice
The built-in PHP web server is not for production use. It may not handle multiple requests as well as the apache web server and may have some security problems that can jeopardize your application or even your host server. Therefore, use it only for development purposes.

The parameter 0.0.0.0 implies that the built-in php server will be listening on all network interfaces and the number 80 directs it to listen on port 80. If you get an error saying that php cannot start listening on port 80, then you can choose another free port, for example 8080, and run the above command with the changed port number.

After the setup is complete, start your browser and point it to the URL of your newly set up ZF2 Skeleton Application. Your screen should look like the image shown below. (Note: if you are using port 8080, the URL should be **http://learnzf2:8080/**)

---

6 http://php.net/manual/en/features.commandline.webserver.php

ZF: Skeleton Application   Home

Welcome to Zend Framework 2

Congratulations! You have successfully installed the ZF2 Skeleton Application. You are currently running Zend Framework version 2.2.1. This skeleton can serve as a simple starting point for you to begin building your application on ZF2.

Fork Zend Framework 2 on GitHub »

Follow Development

Zend Framework 2 is under active development. If you are interested in following the development of ZF2, there is a special ZF2 portal on the official Zend Framework website which provides links to the ZF2 wiki, dev blog, issue tracker, and much more. This is a great resource for staying up to date with the latest developments!

ZF2 Development Portal »

Discover Modules

The community is working on developing a community site to serve as a repository and gallery for ZF2 modules. The project is available on GitHub. The site is currently live and currently contains a list of some of the modules already available for ZF2.

Explore ZF2 Modules »

Help & Support

If you need any help or support while developing with ZF2, you may reach us via IRC: #zftalk on Freenode. We'd love to hear any questions or feedback you may have regarding the beta releases. Alternatively, you may subscribe and post questions to the mailing lists.

Ping us on IRC »

Skeleton Application

The skeleton application is a good example from which to learn. Let's get a closer look at its structure and the most important directories and files.

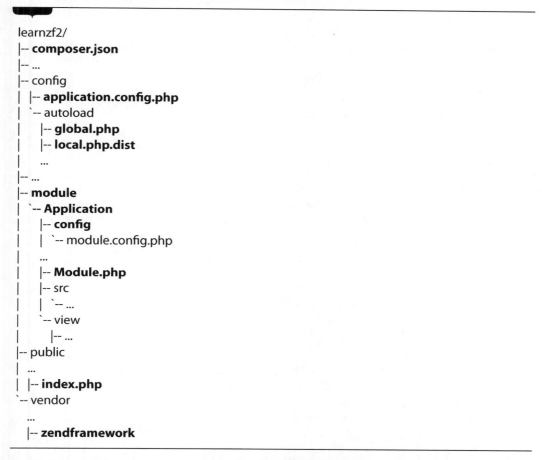

```
learnzf2/
|-- composer.json
|-- ...
|-- config
|   |-- application.config.php
|   `-- autoload
|       |-- global.php
|       |-- local.php.dist
|       ...
|-- ...
|-- module
|   `-- Application
|       |-- config
|       |   `-- module.config.php
|       ...
|       |-- Module.php
|       |-- src
|       |   `-- ...
|       `-- view
|           |-- ...
|-- public
|   ...
|   |-- index.php
`-- vendor
    ...
    |-- zendframework
```

The skeleton application contains the code of our new application with a single module called Application. Every application has one or more application configuration files. Every application consists of one or more modules. Every module has its own configuration. Together the module and application configuration files are consolidated at runtime into the final configuration.

Application Configuration Files

Main Configuration File

The main application configuration file is **config/application.config.php**.

When you open it you will see the following code:

```php
<?php
return array(
  'modules' => array(
    'Application',
  ),
  'module_listener_options' => array(
    'config_glob_paths'   => array(
      'config/autoload/{,*.}{global,local}.php',
    ),
    'module_paths' => array(
      './module',
      './vendor',
    ),
  ),
);
```

The modules key in the array above is used to specify which modules are enabled. At the moment only the Application module is enabled. When we start building other modules into our application we will add their names to the list.

The order in which the module names are added in this array is very important. When application initialization starts, modules are loaded and initialized in the order specified in this array. If we have a module B that is depending on module A, then we have to add A before B in the list.

When the application is started, each module's configuration is retrieved in the order specified in the application configuration file, and is then consolidated in a manner akin to the merging of arrays in PHP[7]. The implications of this are that the next module can override settings from the previous module. In this manner configuration and functionality are extended.

Local and Global Configuration Files

The **config_glob_paths** key in the main application file specifies the location and naming of additional application configuration files which may be loaded. These files should be located under **config/autoload/** and their names should end with global.php or local.php. Although you can change the configuration to use different name patterns, I would advise you to adhere to the default.

The configuration files ending with local.php are used to specify configuration for the current machine. When I talk about a local machine I will be using the term application environment. Application environment is used to specify where the application is running. This could apply to the following server environments:

- **development**: the machine where we develop the application
- **testing**: where we ask bunch of non-technical guys to test our application
- **staging**: where we have a setup that is very close to our live server, or
- **production**: where our application is being used heavily from our customers

One good example for information that should be stored in the local.php configuration files are database or cache parameters.

On the other hand *global.php files are not dependent on the application environment. The *global.php files should include settings that override modules settings currently active. Because these files will be in the git repository you should not include in them sensitive information such as passwords.

---

7 The actual ZF2 merge method differs a bit from array_merge (http://php.net/manual/en/function.array-merge.php) and you can see its code from here: https://github.com/zendframework/zf2/blob/master/library/Zend/Stdlib/ArrayUtils.php#L246-L274

In most cases, local and global configuration file templates will come from modules.

Module Configuration

Module Paths

The module_paths application configuration key specifies the places where our modules are located. The modules that we develop will reside under **module/** and third-party modules will reside under **vendor/**. Our first module **Application** is in module/Application and the ZF2 library code is located under vendor/zendframework.

Main Module Directory

The main configuration file for the Application module is located under module/Application/config/**module.config.php**.

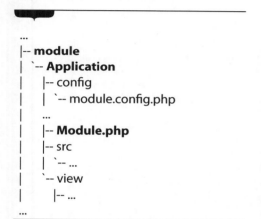

```
...
|-- module
|   `-- Application
|       |-- config
|       |   `-- module.config.php
|       ...
|       |-- Module.php
|       |-- src
|       |   `-- ...
|       `-- view
|           |-- ...
...
```

In this file we will define the capabilities that our module provides, such as services, views, routing, controllers and more. In the directory **module/Application/config/** you can also specify other configuration files, mainly *.local.php.dist and *.global.php.dist files. These describe what can be overridden in this module to tune it for the needs of the of the application environment (*.local.php.dist files) and the application itself (*.global.php.dist files). You should be generous with the comments in these files and describe the purpose of the different parameters. The module user should be instructed, in your comments, to copy these .dist files to the application configuration directory **config/autoload**, where the ".dist" extension should be removed

Here is a little example to illustrate this: A new module will provide database services. In order to configure this service we can create a configuration file module/<ModuleName>/config/database.local.php.dist. If we want to configure database settings, once we enable this module, we have to copy this file to config/autoload and remove the .dist extension of the end. In this manner, our application will be able to load the database configuration settings specifically tuned for the current application environment.

Module.php

The minimal requirement for a module is to have a file named **Module.php**. In it we specify the module configuration and the location of the classes belonging to this module to be autoloaded. The methods in the <ModuleName>\Module class responsible for the configuration and autoloading are called **getConfig** and **getAutoloaderConfig** respectively. These methods, defined in the skeleton app, do not need to be changed and probably the only method where you will have to add code is in the **onBootstrap** method. This is the method that is called after all modules are loaded, the application is started, the complete configuration is merged and the module is bootstrapped. It is a quite powerful method and in it we can attach listeners to events, define new routing and put all the code that is needed for every request.

Composer.json

Composer is the PHP tool that we will use to manage our application and dependant modules. Composer.json is the configuration file that describes the application and its requirements. Below is its content.

```
{
  "name": "zendframework/skeleton-application",
  "description": "Skeleton Application for ZF2",
  "license": "BSD-3-Clause",
  "keywords": [
    "framework",
    "zf2"
  ],
  "homepage": "http://framework.zend.com/",
  "require": {
    "php": ">=5.3.3",
    "zendframework/zendframework": "2.*"
  }
}
```

At the moment the important fields for us are "name" and "require". The first describes the unique name of our application or module and the second one describes the modules that our application needs to have in order to work. The name consists of vendor prefix, something that should be short and at the same time descriptive of you or your company. The second part is the unique name that describes what the module is supposed to do.

The items on which our application depends are php version 5.3.3 or later and Zend Framework version 2. Later in the book we will take a deeper look at this file and the composer tool.

The Public Directory

The public directory and all of its files and subdirectories will be the only entries directly accessible from the web browser. This is the directory where you should copy CSS, images or JavaScript files. You must not put in that directory any sensitive data such as user credentials or credit card numbers.

The public directory contains the **index.php** file. All requests from the web browser are directed to this file. You should keep this file as light as possible as it will be executed in every request. This is the file where the ZF2 engine is loaded and run.

In this book we will not be making changes to this file.

Now that we have discussed initial information about the most important files in the skeleton application, we can start talking about the application that we will be building during the course of the book.

Our Application

What we will be building together is our Training Center Application or TC for short. Our first module will be the Debug module. It will help us get a better understanding of the inner workings of our application. Then we will create a module called User that will handle user management. Finally we will add an Exam module that will be responsible for listing and taking exams.

With every new module we will demonstrate how the different ZF2 components can best be used to continuously improve our application.

First Code Modification

Let's get ready to do some coding and make our first modification to the TC application.

First we will create a welcome page for our TC application that will reuse the existing welcome page from the skeleton application. Open the file **index. phtml** located under <path-to-application>/module/Application/view/application/index/ as shown in the image below

This file contains most of the HTML that you saw when you first opened the skeleton application in the browser. This file is located under the /module/Application/view directory which is the directory where the module HTML files will be stored. We will call these files view templates. They must contain only the logic needed for the visual rendering of the page. The idea is that even a web designer with no knowledge of PHP or Zend Framework 2 should be able, with a bit of effort, to do his or her job. The file extension "phtml" indicates that we have a HTML file with PHP in it. At the top of the index.phtml view template there is this code:

```
<h1><?php echo sprintf($this->translate('Welcome to %sZend Framework 2%s'), '<span class="zf-green">', '</span>') ?></h1>
```

This is the text we will be using for our welcome page. Since all of you are familiar with PHP then you know that the part enclosed between <?php and ?> tags is PHP code. In this code we are calling normal built-in functions from PHP as well as custom methods that will help us with the visual presentation of the data. The call $this->translate(...) utilizes logic called a **view helper** that translates the text given as a parameter to the current language of the application.

Next we will replace the complete text in the index.phtml file with the following code:

```
<div class="hero-unit">
  <h1><?php
    echo sprintf($this->translate('Welcome to %s<br>'), "Training Center");
    echo sprintf($this->translate('version: %s'), '0.0.1') ?></h1>
</div>
```

If you go back to the browser and refresh the content of your application you will see output similar to what is shown below:

ZF: Skeleton Application   Home

Welcome to Training Center version: 0.0.1

Arguably the sexiest welcome page of a ZF2 project, we will leave the styling in the hands of graphic designers so that they can produce an award-winning look and feel! What we did in the view was to hard code the name of the application and its version. Hard-coding data is a bad idea in general, and we will try to have this information derived from a better source.

ZF2 uses the MVC design pattern. According to the definition in Wikipedia "*In software engineering, a design pattern is a general reusable solution to a commonly occurring problem within a given context in software design.*"[8]. MVC stands for Model View Controller and we have already started talking about views. The MVC pattern provides a solution as to how to separate presentation logic from controller logic, and how to combine it with the business data appropriate to your application. We will be discussing this pattern in more detail later in the book.

We edited the file index.phtml under the directory .../view/application/**index**. In ZF2 terms, this means that we edited the view template (index.phtml, which matches the name of the controller action), for the index controller (which matches the name of the directory where the index.phtml file is located).

Pertinent to a discussion of MVC, the controller in our application is the place where we pass information, like the application name and version, to the view. Open the file IndexController.php that is located under <path-to-application>/model/Application/src/Application/Controller/, like shown on the image below:

8 http://en.wikipedia.org/wiki/Software_design_pattern

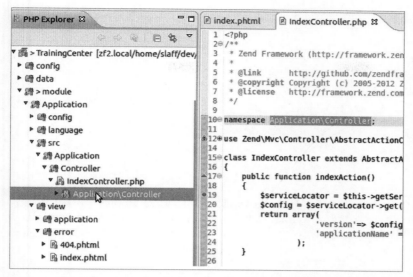

The class that can be found in Index-Controller.php contains a public method named indexAction. From this method we will be able to pass information processed by the index.phtml view template. In ZF2 the easiest way to pass information to the view is to return an associative array. The keys of the array will be the names of the view variables and the values will be the data that is visualized. Let's change the code of the indexAction method as follows:

```php
public function indexAction()
{
    return array('version'=> '0.0.1', 'applicationName'=> "Training Center");
}
```

We have now passed data from the controller to the view, but in the view we still have hard coded values. In order to display them we will have to change the view template code with this:

```php
<div class="hero-unit">
  <h1><?php
    echo sprintf($this->translate('Welcome to %s<br>'), $this->applicationName);
    echo sprintf($this->translate('version: %s'), $this->version) ?></h1>
</div>
```

The application name and version number are already configuration options, which means they do not have to be hard-coded in the controller. All we need to do is to have the controller read them from the config service, one of the services that is assigned by default in Zend Framework 2. For now think of services as objects that provide you with business data and business logic. In order to get access to the config service you can rewrite indexAction as shown below:

```php
public function indexAction()
{
    $serviceLocator = $this->getServiceLocator();
    $config = $serviceLocator->get('config');
    return array(
        'version'=> $config['application']['version'],
        'applicationName' => $config['application']['name']
    );
}
```

After first retrieving the service locator, from it we can get the config service. The config service is an array containing the final merged configuration of our application and all of its modules.

Before we declare this first small task "finished with great success" we will have to add the actual configuration information into the config files. We will use the module config file of the Application module. Open the <path-to-application>/module/Application/config/module.config.php and add a new associative array key called "application" with sub-keys for name and version. Try to do it yourself using the image below as a guide.

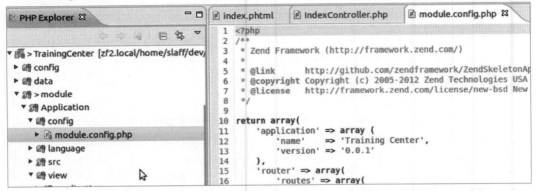

If you go back to your browser now and reload the welcome page you will see that the new page looks suspiciously similar to the previous one. Your suspicions are correct! The visual presentation is the same: the only difference is that we have logically separated the data from the view in the correct places.

First Controller Action

Editing an already existing action and view is a good start, but the more we wish to achieve, the more code we will need. Now we will create a new action in the index controller that will be called **about**. This action will output information about the purpose of the Training Center Application. To create this action create a new method in the IndexController class and name it **aboutAction**.

The naming is important. The first part of the method name represents how we will call our action and the Action postfix is added to signify that this method can be used as an action in our controller. We will not pass any information from our about action to the view. The following code will be sufficient.

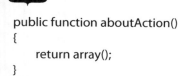

```
public function aboutAction()
{
    return array();
}
```

The information to be visualized will come from the view template, which we need to create. For that we will need to create a new file called **about. phtml** and save it in the <path-to-application>/ module/Application/view/application/index/ directory. We save it here because the *about* action is part of the index controller. If the controller was named **company**, for example, then we would save it under the <path-to-application>/module/Application/view/application/company/ folder.

Open about.phtml and paste in text from the beginning of this chapter where it is explained what our application will be doing. Then go to your browser and as the URI part of the URL type /application/index/about. The complete URL should be something like http://localhost/application/index/about. Once this URL is requested ZF2 will use technique called routing that will try to map the URL to a controller and action. Luckily we already have route that helps us to direct URIs like **/application/<controller-name>/<action-name>** to their respective module, controller and action. And as a result we should see a page with information about our Training Center application.

This is how we got our feet wet in the exciting pond full of new knowledge called Zend Framework 2. In the following chapter I will give you more insight about the inner workings of ZF2.

If your code did not work as expected or you are just curious to see the solution for this chapter then type the following sequence of commands:

```
cd <full/path/to/>/learnzf2/

# If you have local changes use git add <file> or git rm <file> to add them or remove them

# Do not add the files under the vendor/ folder to the repository.

git stash # This is used to stash your local changes

git checkout 'ch-first-controller'
```

How Zend Framework 2 Works

The diagram describing the sequence flow of a typical ZF2 application can look as complex as the diagram below.

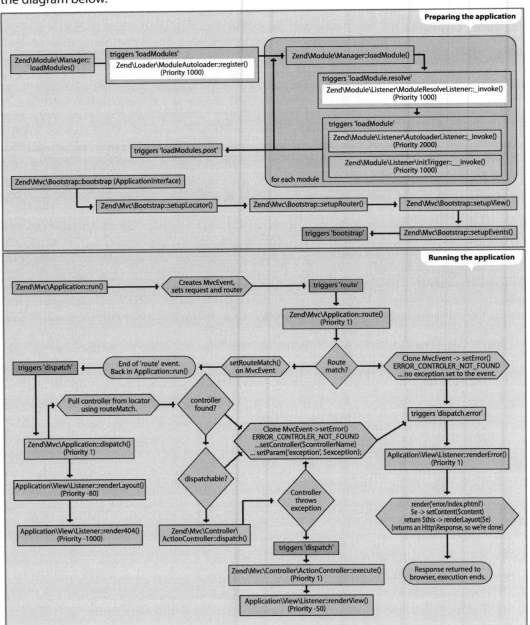

Initially we will limit ourselves to the major parts of this diagram in order to explain how Zend Framework works. When the user makes a request from the web browser the first file that is executed is index.php. It loads the main ZF2 engine and continues execution in two consecutive phases: the **preparation** phase and the **running** phase.

In the preparation phase the application and all enabled modules are loaded. The ZF2 engine marks the end of a step and the beginning of a new step by emitting messages with a specific unique name. These messages in Zend Framework 2 are called events and the act of emitting a message is called triggering. The events in the preparation phase are "loadModules", "loadModule.resolve", "loadModule" and "loadModules.post".

- **loadModules** is triggered when the loading of the modules starts. Autoloaders usually listen for this event.

- **loadModule.resolve** is executed for each enabled module. When "loadModule.resolve" is triggered the listeners for this event try to produce from the module name an instance of the Module class.

- **loadModule** is also triggered for each enabled module, once the module name is resolved to an object. At that moment the **init** method in the module is called.

- **loadModules.post** is triggered at the end when all modules are loaded. It is used to allow the modules to do some extra work. For example "loadModules.post" can be used to prepare the infrastructure for the module, such as creating a database as the module first loads, or creating data and cache directories with the correct permissions.

During the preparation phase all module configuration files are loaded and merged with the application configuration files to form the final configuration. The end of the preparation phase is marked with the triggering of the "bootstrap" event. This causes the **onBootstrap** method in every loaded module to be called. In the onBootstrap method we can attach our event listeners.

The preparation phase is followed by the running phase in which the Model-View-Controller (MVC) logic starts. Events triggered during this phase include "route", "dispatch", "render" and "finish".

- **route** is triggered first. The routing process reads the request parameters, such as method, URI, GET or POST parameters, and provides information about the module, controller and action that need to be loaded.

- **dispatch** is triggered when the action starts execution.

- **render** is triggered next if the application dictates visualizing the results.

- **finish** is triggered last.

In simple terms, these two phases are how a ZF2 application works. In order to have a better overeall picture, however, we will also need to investigate the major components of Zend Framework 2.

Creating a Debug Module

In order to explore the work flow in Zend Framework 2 and engage your interest, we will create our first module. The name of the module should be simple and descriptive. For the purposes of the book we will name our first module "Debug".

Manual Module Creation

Zend Framework 2 does not limit you to use any specific code editor or Integrated Development Environment (IDE). As long as you are fine with copying and pasting files and folders you can easily create your first module manually. You can copy the /module/Application/ directory to a new directory called /module/Debug and replace all occurrences of Application with Debug. The replacement has to be done for file names, in the namespace declaration and in the module configuration file. This is an error prone process and you have to be careful when replacing. When done, your directory structure should be similar to the following:

```
Debug/
|-- config
|   `-- module.config.php
|-- language
|-- Module.php
|-- src
|   `-- Debug
|       `-- Controller
|           `-- IndexController.php
`-- view
    |-- debug
    |   `-- index
    |       |-- index.phtml
```

Your module.config.php file should look as follows:

```php
<?php

return array(
    'router' => array(
        'routes' => array(
            'home' => array(
                'type' => 'Zend\Mvc\Router\Http\Literal',
                'options' => array(
                    'route'   => '/',
                    'defaults' => array(
                        'controller' => 'Debug\Controller\Index',
                        'action'   => 'index',
                    ),
                ),
            ),
```

```php
        // Simply drop new controllers in, and you can access them
            // using the path /debug/:controller/:action
        'debug' => array(
            'type'   => 'Literal',
            'options' => array(
                'route'   => '/debug',
                'defaults' => array(
                    '__NAMESPACE__' => 'Debug\Controller',
                    'controller'   => 'Index',
                    'action'       => 'index',
                ),
            ),
            'may_terminate' => true,
            'child_routes' => array(
                'default' => array(
                    'type'   => 'Segment',
                    'options' => array(
                        'route'   => '/[:controller[/:action]]',
                        'constraints' => array(
                            'controller' => '[a-zA-Z][a-zA-Z0-9_-]*',
                            'action'    => '[a-zA-Z][a-zA-Z0-9_-]*',
                        ),
                        'defaults' => array(
                        ),
                    ),
                ),
            ),
        ),
    ),
),
'service_manager' => array(
    'factories' => array(
    ),
),
'controllers' => array(
    'invokables' => array(
        'Debug\Controller\Index' => 'Debug\Controller\IndexController'
    ),
),
'view_manager' => array(
    'template_path_stack' => array(
__DIR__ . '/../view',
    ),
),
);
```

If you compare this config file with the one from the application module you will see that we removed also the "translate" definition as it is not needed for the Debug module. Once you are finished creating the module you will have to enable it. This is done by editing the application configuration file <path-to-application>/config/application.config.php and adding the Debug entry as a value under the "modules" key. Example code is shown below:

```php
<?php
return array(
  'modules' => array(
    'Application',
    'Debug',
  ),
  'module_listener_options' => array(
    'config_glob_paths'   => array(
      'config/autoload/{,*.}{global,local}.php',
    ),
    'module_paths' => array(
      './module',
      './vendor',
    ),
  ),
);
```

Automatic Module Creation (with ZFtool)

If you want to work mostly from the command line, then you can download "zftool" and use it to create your ZF2 module. In order to get a copy of the tool, go to the Zend Framework 2 packages website and download the phar file from there. The following command should do the work for you:

```
cd <full/path/to/>/learnzf2/
wget https://packages.zendframework.com/zftool.phar
```

Once it is downloaded you can start using it right away. Creating a module is as simple as running the following command:

```
php zftool.phar create module Debug
```

Debug is the module name. If you want to create modules with another name just replace Debug from the command above with the desired module name.

Automatic Module Creation (with Zend Studio)

Another way to create a new module is to use the automated features from Zend Studio version 10 or newer. Zend Studio is an IDE[9] based on Eclipse and focused on development with PHP and Zend Framework. You can download it from the Zend Technologies website[10] and use it for free[11] during the time you are reading this book.

---

9 http://www.zend.com/en/products/studio/

10 http://www.zend.com/en/products/studio/downloads

11 The trial period is 30 days. During that period you can use all its features. After that some of the features will be disabled.

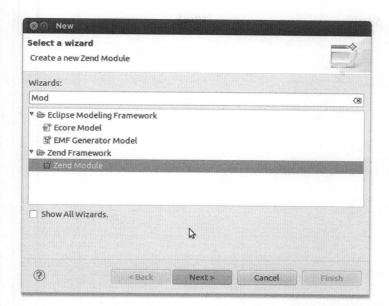

Once you have your TC project in Zend Studio you can enable ZF2 support, if you haven't done this already. Right click on you project -> Configure -> Enable Zend Framework Support. Choose version 2.x. After that right click on your project and select New -> Other and from the list of possible wizards choose Zend Module. The image below is for orientation.

You can then follow the instructions given by the wizard. Remember to put Debug as module name, as shown in the picture below:

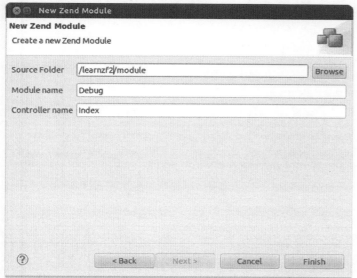

Once you create the new module it will automatically be enabled in the application configuration file.

Coding Our First Module.php

What we will do now is to edit the Module.php file created for the Debug module. We will add a "listener" to the loadModules.post event. This particular event is triggered when all modules for our application have been loaded. The listener will then collect information about the modules loaded.

Open the <path-to-application>/module/Debug/Module.php file and in the module class add a public method **init**. The init method is called during the initialization of the module. It receives as an argument the module manager instance. From it we can get the event manager. We will use the latter to attach a listener to the loadModules.post event. (If you are in doubt why I have chosen this event please review the the previous chapter!) And finally in the callback that handles the event we will print the loaded modules in the event log. The code of the module should look similar to the following:

```php
<?php
namespace Debug;

use Zend\ModuleManager\Feature\AutoloaderProviderInterface;
use Zend\Mvc\ModuleRouteListener;
use Zend\ModuleManager\ModuleManager;
use Zend\EventManager\Event;

class Module implements AutoloaderProviderInterface
{
    public function init(ModuleManager $moduleManager)
    {
        $eventManager = $moduleManager->getEventManager();
        $eventManager->attach('loadModules.post', array($this, 'loadedModulesInfo'));
    }

    public function loadedModulesInfo(Event $event)
    {
        $moduleManager = $event->getTarget();
        $loadedModules = $moduleManager->getLoadedModules();
        error_log(var_export($loadedModules, true));
    }
}
```

Run the changed code in the browser and on every new request in the error log of the web server you will see how many modules are loaded and their names. This is helpful for debugging purposes and exactly the type of thing our Debug module should do.

If you had difficulty entering the source code changes above then you can run the following sequence of commands.

```
cd <full/path/to/>/learnzf2/
git stash # Stash your local changes
git checkout 'ch-debug-module'
```

In the PHP code above we dove a bit deeper into the ZF2 pond, covering the event manager and module manager. These managers are part of the major components described in the next chapter. Before we get to that point, however, let's take a look at best practices for the Module. php file.

Best Practice

Keep the init and onBootstrap methods from the Module.php as light as possible. It is a good practice to register listeners for events here, but not to instantiate resources such as setting up a database adapter or initializing cache. The reason for this is that these methods are called on every execution, whereas a database adapter, for example, may be required only on some of the pages. Therefore it makes more sense to instantiate the database resource via the service manager, which is elaborated in later chapters.

If the module has to create directories or files to write data (e.g. cache data), then always put these directories or files **outside** of the module directory tree. A good place for writes would be under <full/path/to/>/learnzf2/data/*. The reason for this is that later you can more easily keep your module up-to-date using tools like composer.

Keep your module configuration files as simple and as short as possible. This file is loaded on every request and merged with the other module config files. If a module does not need to present any information for display, then you can remove all routes, controllers and view definitions.

In the coming chapter I will add additional best practices related to modules and their configuration.

Modular Architecture

Modular architecture "*refers to the design of any system composed of separate components that can be connected together. The beauty of modular architecture is that you can replace or add any one component (module) without affecting the rest of the system. The opposite of a modular architecture is an integrated architecture, in which no clear divisions exist between components*"[12] . A module is *"a self-contained unit or item that can be combined or interchanged with others like it to create different shapes or designs"*.[13]

A true ZF2 application has a modular architecture. An application can contain one or more modules. There are several rules you should apply in order to define a good module. Some of them come directly from the definition of a module or of modular architecture:

Module Should ...	Discussion
Be self-contained	A module must have functionality integral to its operation completely contained inside of its own module code-base. If the functionality is spread across other modules that usually do not depend on each other, then you have created sub optimal module. In order to test if your module is self contained, the application as a whole should continue to function normally regardless of whether you enable or disable the module at any point during the development process. (Given that, if you were to disable the module, the functionality of the module would not be available to the application, of course!)
Have a clear purpose	Do not write modules that cover areas which are not logically connected. For example, if you create a Debug module, put only functionality that helps you to debug the application. Do not create a module that does a lot of things but has no clear purpose. Such modules are very hard to reuse in other applications. In order to test if your module has a clear purpose, at any given moment you should be able to come up with a short statement of its purpose.
Implement logically grouped functionality	A module is a complete solution to a discrete problem or set of related problems. If you have a User module, for example, you should only define functionality related to user managerment, authentication and access control. Do not place in this module functionality that improves the navigation or the layout of the application: this would represent functionality which is not logically related to user management.

---

12 http://www.webopedia.com/TERM/M/modular_architecture.html
13 http://www.thefreedictionary.com/modular

Be simple to use and to extend	It should be as simple as possible to start using a module. Any changes needed to make the module work should be limited to configuration changes and added functionality. Changes that require a rewrite of core classes from the module indicate a poorly programmed module. In order to test if your module is simple to use and to extend, ask yourself how many configuration changes would be needed, and how many core classes would have to be overridden, in order to use the module. If the number of configuration changes is excessive, or the number core classes which must be overridden is more than 2, then something is wrong.
Allow loose coupling	You have provided loose coupling if disabling this module does not break the other modules (assuming there is no module which depends on this one). Modules should only exchange messages (events in ZF2 terms) in order to communicate with each other. If a module depends on another, the dependency should mainly involve services that it uses. In order to test if your module allows loose coupling, you should ask yourself if another module will be able to interact with it, and to extend its functionality, using only events.

A successful implantation of these rules depends on the ZF2 capabilities on one hand and on the skill of the developer on the other hand. The good news is that ZF2 has all components needed to implement a good module. The next paragraphs describe them.

Major Components

Module Manager

The module manager is one of the components that is used in our code above. It is responsible for loading modules and keeping information about them. It is one of the most important ZF2 engine components, making it possible for modules to start running. Most of the time, you will not work with the module manager directly. One exception, however, would be to add pre or post configuration steps to your module or to gather debug information about the modules, as we did in the previous chapter. The official ZF2 documentation has more, albeit sparse, information[14] about the module manager.

If you were to review the Module.php file for the Debug module from the previous chapter, you would notice that a module manager instance is always passed as an argument to the init method. In the init method we wanted to attach listeners that listen for module events. In order to accomplish this, we gained access to the event manager, as shown below:

```
$eventManager = $moduleManager->getEventManager();
```

Once we had the event manager we were able to attach our listeners with this line.

```
$eventManager->attach('loadModules.post', array($this, 'loadedModulesInfo'));
```

The first parameter 'loadModules.post' of the attach method is the unique event name that we want to listen to. The second parameter can be any valid PHP callback[15]. In our case it is array($this, 'loadedModulesInfo'), which represents a callback to the method 'loadedModulesInfo' from the current class.

As we are discussing events, it is time to take a look at this next major component in ZF2.

Events and Event Manager

ZF2 has an event driven architecture. This means that the flow of the application depends on events and when an important change in the application occurs a corresponding event is triggered. The event triggering may carry additional information. There can be zero or more event listeners. Usually the event is passed to all listeners for this event. When one of the event listeners finishes processing the event data it may prevent the other pending event listeners from further processing.

Having an event-driven architecture allows the ZF2 application to be loosely coupled and thus very extensible. Let's give an example of this: in a framework with non-event driven architecture, like Zend Framework 1, when an error occurs during dispatch we can handle it using the following pseudo-code:

14 http://framework.zend.com/manual/2.0/en/modules/zend.module-manager.module-manager.html#zend-mod-ule-manager-module-manager
15 http://php.net/manual/en/language.types.callable.php

```php
public function errorAction()
{
    $errorData = $this->getErrorData();
    if (APPLICATION_ENV=='DEBUG') {
        $errorData = $this->processData($errorData);
        // pass the data to the view visualization
        $this->view = $errorData;
    }

    // ...
}
```

Now if we also want to add error logging, we would have to modify this method and add the following lines:

```php
public function errorAction()
{
    $errorData = $this->getErrorData();
    if (APPLICATION_ENV=='DEBUG') {
        $errorData = $this->processData($errorData);
        // pass the data to the view visualization
        $this->view = $errorData;
    }

    $this->logger->err("Got error data:".var_export($errorData,true));

    // ...
}
```

Further, if we wanted to send an email when a critical event occurs, such as a database error, we would have to modify the source code again. And what shall we do if we want to add new module that overrides the errorAction that must send an email on database error and also text message? You guessed it: we would have to write the new errorAction with repeated code from the previous errorAction! Now we have duplicate code, making it more difficult to reuse and maintain.

In ZF2 with its event driven architecture it is much simpler to write code which can then easily be reused. Because the ZF2 triggers the "dispatch.error" event in case of an error in our modules, we can add listeners to this event and log the data or send it to an email. At any time we can extend the error handling code just by adding new event listener. In order to see the difference I will show you how to add event listener to the dispatch.error that writes information into the error log.

Open the Module.php file of the Debug module. Replace the onBootstrap method with the following code:

```php
public function onBootstrap(MvcEvent $e)
{
    $eventManager    = $e->getApplication()->getEventManager();
    $eventManager->attach(MvcEvent::EVENT_DISPATCH_ERROR, array($this, 'handleError'));
}

public function handleError(MvcEvent $event)
{
    $controller = $event->getController();
    $error    = $event->getParam('error');
    $exception = $event->getParam('exception');
    $message = 'Error:'.$error;
    if ($exception instanceof \Exception) {
        $message .= ', Exception('.$exception->getMessage().'): '.
            $exception->getTraceAsString();
    }

    error_log($message);

}
```

In the code above, the callback we attached to the "dispatch.error" event is the handleError method in the same class. Notice that I used the class constant MvcEvent::EVENT_DISPATCH_ ERROR to specify the event name. It is a best practice to use the constants instead of directly typing the event name.

In handleError, from the event object, we can get information, about the error and, if it has an exception associated with it, the exception instance. Check the code in your browser by adding the following URL http://localhost/non-existent-path. This must report an error with the routing in the error log.

If you had difficulties running the code above you can review the solution provided for this chapter. Run the following sequence of commands:

```
cd <full/path/to/>/learnzf2/
# Use git add or git rm to add or delete your local changes, if any
git stash ; You should know by now why you do this – to stash your local changes
git checkout 'ch-events'
```

Triggering Events

In ZF2 you can also trigger your own events. Triggering an event can be done from anywhere in your code and is as simple as calling the following lines of code:

```
use Zend\EventManager\EventManager;

$event = new EventManager('channel-25');
$event->trigger('new song', null, array('artist'=> 'Adele'));
```

What we did here is to create new event manager. The event manager constructor in ZF2 accepts "id" as an argument and in our case the value of the id is 'channel-25'. I chose this name on purpose. The id is like a radio channel that you can tune into. You can then send or listen to events over that channel. What we did above is to send the event 'new song' with an array with one parameter as the third argument.

Listening to Events

Once we have sent the event, let's see how we can listen to it. One of the most common places where we will be listening to events in our modules is in the onBootstrap method in the Module.php file. Listening to events requires us to access the Shared Event Manager.

> **Notice**
> Using the following code to listen to events on the specific id will not work!
>
> ```
> $eventManager = new EventManager();
> $eventManager->attach('channel-25','new song', function(Event $event) {
>         $artist = $event->getParam('artist');
>         error_log('Got new song from artist:'.$artist);
> });
> ```
>
> You need to get access to the SharedEventManager and from it listen to events happening on 'channel-25'

You may say: "*Well why not just attach it to the $eventManager instance like we did with the 'dispatch.error' event*"? Take a look at the top of the onBootstrap method again and you may find the answer yourself.

```
public function onBootstrap(MvcEvent $e)
{
    $eventManager    = $e->getApplication()->getEventManager();
    $eventManager->attach('MvcEvent::EVENT_DISPATCH_ERROR', array($this, 'handleError'));
```

The $eventManager is actually only for MVC events. Therefore we cannot listen to our new event with it. In the onBootstrap method in the Module.php file we can gain access to the shared event manager and listen to our event using the following code.

```
public function onBootstrap(MvcEvent $event)
{
        $eventManager = $event->getApplication()->getEventManager();
        $sharedEventManager = $eventManager->getSharedManager();
        $sharedEventManager->attach('channel-25','new song', function(Event $event) {
            $artist = $event->getParam('artist');
            error_log('Got new song from artist:'.$artist);
        });
        // ....
}
```

The attach method accepts id as the first parameter, event name as the second and callback as the third. If we want to listen to the 'new-song' event on all channels we can specify the value '*' for the id parameter, as you can see below:

```
//...
$sharedEventManager->attach('*','new song', function(Event $event) {
//..
```

If we want to just listen on selected channels, then we can pass an array to the id parameter, as follows:

```
//...
$sharedEventManager->attach(array('jazz','romantic','channel-25'),
                    'new song',
                    function(Event $event) {
//..
```

The same applies also for the event name. If you want to listen to all events on the selected channels pass '*' as an event name, or if you want only to listen to the events 'new song','traffic information' and 'news', you can pass an array as shown below:

```
//...
$sharedEventManager->attach(array('jazz','romantic','channel-25'),
                    array('new song','traffic information','news'),
                    function(Event $event) {
//..
```

The attach method has a fourth parameter which is the priority of the listener. Priority is represented by an integer. The bigger the integer value the higher the priority. Positive numbers are used for event listeners that will be executed first and negative numbers for event listeners that will be executed last. If you do not specify a priority, then the default value of one will be used. For example ZF2 by default triggers a MVC event called "route" which signals the routing process. If we want to check after the routing if the current user has the permissions to go to this page then we can attach an event listener with priority -100, for example. We will use this fact later in the book to build our access control module.

One interesting thing about event listeners is the fact that you can short-circuit them. What this means is that from an event listener you can prevent the execution of any further event listeners. As an example, let's say you have two event listeners. In the callback for the first event listener that is executed you write something like this:

```
// ...
$sharedEventManager->attach('*','new song', function(Event $event) {
    // ...
    $event->stopPropagation(true);
    // ..
    // notice:
    // unless you return, all remaining code in the  callback will be executed
}
```

In this example, the callback for the second event listener will never be called!

Can you now predict what will happen in the code below? (Hint: from your browser enter the application URL and add extra random symbols at the end to deliberately generate an error.)

```
public function onBootstrap(MvcEvent $e)
{
    $eventManager     = $e->getApplication()->getEventManager();
    $eventManager->attach(
        'MvcEvent::EVENT_DISPATCH_ERROR',
        function(MvcEvent $event) {
            error_log($event->getParam('error'));
            $event->stopPropagation(true);
        },
        100);
}
```

As you can see, before this event listener was added, the web page displayed error information. After we added this listener the information is no longer shown because our listener has a priority of 100, which will be executed before the standard code for "dispatch.error". Additionally, we stopped the event propagation, which means that subsequent event listeners for this event will not be executed at all. Accordingly, we did not see any error information in the web page. If you did not come to the same conclusion, please take time to review this section before continuing with your reading.

Another interesting aspect of event triggering is that you can not only specify logic to be executed after every execution of the listeners, but you can also prevent the execution of further event listeners from a specific point. This is done by passing a PHP callback as fourth parameter to the event **trigger** method

```
$event = new EventManager('channel-25');
$event->trigger('new song', null, array('artist'=> 'Adele'), function($result){
    // if the result matches our criteria
    // then we can short-circuit the execution by returning 1 or true as shown below
    if ($result == 'stop') { // result is the returned value from
        // the event listener that is being executed now
        return true;
    }
});
```

With that we completed our introduction to events and event managers. For a complete list of the ZF2 engine events with explanation about them take a look at the official reference manual[16].

Service Manager

The service manager is another major component of ZF2. You might notice the term Service Locator in the ZF2 source code or documentation. It is practically the same as Sevice Manager.

Service Manager is a type of intelligent registry where you give it a simple string key and receive in return an instance of the class that was defined in your application. For example if you need the config service you can simply make the following call:

```
$serviceManager->get('config')
```

If there is no definition for the 'config' service an exception will be thrown. If there is a definition, but no instance is currently available then the service manager will create one for you.

In ZF2 you can define a service in multiple ways. The convention which will be used in this book will be to define them only in the module config file. We will do this because it improves the readability of our module. Using this approach, we can easily see what services our module is overriding and what new services is our module providing to the complete application.

Defining Services

Services in the Service Manager can only be arrays or objects: defining anything else as a service, such as a scalar, will throw an exception. If you open the module config file for the Application module (module/Application/config/module.config.php) you will see a definition similar to this:

```
'service_manager' => array(
    'factories' => array(
        'translator' => 'Zend\I18n\Translator\TranslatorServiceFactory',
    ),
),
```

The 'service_manager' key is used to define various services. Services can be defined in several different ways. The keys immediately under the 'service_manager' key define the way in which we want to initialize our service. We will mention only the most frequently used types: **invokables, factories, initializers, aliases** and **shared**.

---

16 http://framework.zend.com/manual/2.2/en/modules/zend.mvc.mvc-event.html#order-of-events

Invokables definition

You should define an invokable service as an array where the key is the unique name of the service that you want to specify, and the value is the fully qualified class name what will be used to instantiate the service. Consider the following definition in the config file:

```
'service_manager' => array(
    'invokables' => array(
        'log' => 'My\Log\ClassName'
    )
)
```

When this service is called using the syntax $serviceManager->get('log'), it is the equivalent of creating an instance of the class using code similar to this:

```
$name = 'My\Log\ClassName' ;
$logInstance = new $name();
return $logInstance
```

Let's create our first invokables service definition. We will do so in the Debug module configuration file. Our service name will be 'timer' and it will point to Debug\Service\Timer. The definition should look like this:

```
'service_manager' => array(
    'invokables' => array(
        'timer' => 'Debug\Service\Timer'
    )
),
```

The timer class will be saved under the newly created directory module/Debug/src/Debug/Service with a filename of Timer.php. The code of the timer module will be as follows:

```php
<?php
namespace Debug\Service;

/**
 * Simple class that measures the time between start and stop calls.
 * @author slaff
 *
 */
class Timer
{
    /**
     * Start times.
     * @var array
     */
    protected $start;
    /**
```

```
 * Defines if the time must be presented as float
 * @var boolean
 */
protected $timeAsFloat;

public function __construct($timeAsFloat=false)
{
    $this->timeAsFloat = $timeAsFloat;
}

/**
 * Starts measuring the time.
 *
 * @param string $key
 */
public function start($key)
{
    $this->start[$key] = microtime($this->timeAsFloat);
}

/**
 * Stops measuring the time and returns the duration.
 *
 * @param string $key
 * @return float|null the duration of the event
 */
public function stop($key)
{
    if (!isset($this->start[$key])) {
        return null;
    }

    return microtime($this->timeAsFloat) - $this->start[$key];
}
}
```

The invokables service definition will be perfectly sufficient if we do not want to pass arguments to the constructor of the Debug\Service\Timer class or to interact easily with other services. The definition that does allow this interactivity is called 'factories'. Therefore we will change our service definition and learn what the factories definition has to offer.

Factories Definition

When you define a service as a factory you need to add it as a key/value pair under the sevice_ manager -> factories array. The value part of the key/value pair should specify a fully qualified class name that implements Zend\ServiceManager\FactoryInterface, provide name of a class or anonymous function[17]. The latter should be used only for fast development and testing of concepts, but never as part of the final code. There can be problems when using anonymous

17 http://php.net/manual/en/functions.anonymous.php

functions, also known as closures. Below I will list some of them:

1. Configuration caching will break.
   PHP cannot serialize and deserialize closures. Thus, if you decide at some point to cache your final merged configuration, this will not work.
2. The autoloading may not work as expected.
   The code in the closure can depend on a class associated with the next module to be enabled. This means that the class cannot be autoloaded and your code in the closure will break. It can get event worse: The autoloading from the next modules may override the autoloading of a class from the current module. For the whole application the expectation can be that the overridden class is loaded but what will happen is that the current class will be loaded which may lead to problems which are difficult to trace.
3. Performance may decrease.

If you define a service using a closure in the configuration file, then PHP will spend processing time and memory to evaluate it. If there is another module that overwrites this service then the processing time and memory will be lost.

Therefore think twice if you want to use closures. At the time of this writing there are a lot of examples in Internet that use closures, but most of them have the pitfalls listed above.

Now lets change our 'timer' definition from invokables to factories.The service name will be "timer" as before, however we will move this key to factories from invokables and it will use the Debug\Service\Factory\Timer class that we will create. The definition of this service in our module config file can look like this:

```
'service_manager' => array(
    'factories' => array(
        'timer' => 'Debug\Service\Factory\Timer'
    )
),
```

After that change we have to create the service factory class. It has to be saved under the newly created Debug\Service\Factory directory and with the name Timer.php.

The initial content of the factory will be as follows:

```php
<?php
namespace Debug\Service\Factory;

use Zend\ServiceManager\FactoryInterface;
use Zend\ServiceManager\ServiceLocatorInterface;

use Debug\Service\Timer as TimerService;

class Timer implements FactoryInterface
{
    public function createService(ServiceLocatorInterface $serviceLocator)
    {
        $timer = new TimerService();
        return $timer;
    }
}
```

As you can see from the code above, we have to implement one method called createService which receives as a parameter an instance of the service locator. Now if we want to pass a parameter to the constructor we can do it in this method either by hard coding it here, or better by getting it from another service.

The only service we have used so far is the config service. We will use it again to get the parameter that we need to pass to the Timer class. Our createService method will start looking like this:

```
public function createService(ServiceLocatorInterface $serviceLocator)
{
    $config = $serviceLocator->get('config');
    $timer = new TimerService($config['timer']['times_as_float']);
    return $timer;
}
```

What is left is to change the Debug module configuration file and add the following entry in the big configuration array:

```
'timer' => array (
    'times_as_float' => true,
)
```

We now have a service that can be used and set up relatively easy.

Aliases Definition

The aliases definition is used to represent an already existing service definition with another name. Let's say you want to use the 'timer' definition and present it also as 'Debug\Timer'. In order to do this, you would add the following lines into your module configuration file:

```
'service_manager' => array(
   'aliases' => array(
       'Debug\Timer' => 'timer',
   )
```

If you want to get the source code typethe by now familiar sequence of commands:

```
cd <full/path/to/>/learnzf2/
git stash
git checkout 'ch-service-timer'
```

Shared Services

By default all services are shared. This means that once an instance for a service is created it will be reused throughout the request. If, on the other hand, you want to always have new unique instances when you get a service from the service manager, then you can add it to the service_manager definition under the key shared. A definition for non-shared service 'crypto' looks like this:

```
'service_manager' => array(
    'factories' => array (
      'crypto' => 'Crypto\Service\Factory'
    ),
    'shared' => array(
        'crypto' => false,
    ),
)
```

Initializing Services

There is one well hidden feature (at least in the official documentation) that allows you to add additional logic following the creation of your services. This feature is called initializers and it is useful in the cases where you need to make simple lazy loading and injection of dependencies to multiple services.

Let's say that we have a lot of database dependent services. We can have these classes implement **Zend\Db\Adapter\AdapterAwareInterface**. A short example is given below:

```
namespace Debug\Model;
use Zend\Db\Adapter\AdapterAwareInterface;
use Zend\Db\Adapter\Adapter;

class Foo implements AdapterAwareInterface
{
    /**
     * @var Adapter
     */
    protected $adapter;

    public function setDbAdapter(Adapter $adapter)
    {
        $this->adapter = $adapter;
    }
}
```

The actual initializer classes must implement Zend\ServiceManager\InitializerInterface, or use closures. The latter must be avoided as much as possible. The reasons against the use of closures are the same as mentioned for the *factories* definition.

The following is the definition of our initializers in the module configuration:

```
'service_manager' => array(
  'initializers' =>  array (
        'User\Service\Initializer\Db',
    )
  ),
)
```

Below is shown the actual implementation of our Db initializer:

```php
<?php
namespace User\Service\Initializer;

use Zend\Db\Adapter\Adapter;
use Zend\Db\Adapter\AdapterAwareInterface;
use Zend\ServiceManager\InitializerInterface;
use Zend\ServiceManager\ServiceLocatorInterface;

class Db implements InitializerInterface
{
        /**
         * Initialize
         *
         * @param $instance
         * @param ServiceLocatorInterface $serviceLocator
         * @return mixed
         */
        public function initialize($instance, ServiceLocatorInterface $serviceLocator)
        {
                if ($instance instanceof use AdapterAwareInterface) {
                        $instance->setDbAdapter($serviceLocator->get('database'));
                }
        }
}
```

With the definition above we have the guarantee that every service that implements the AdapterAwareInterface will have the dependant database adapter instance injected. We will use this option later on in our application when we start working with databases.

Using Services

What we will do now is to combine the techniques discussed in the book so far in order to add new functionality to our debug module. What we will do is to calculate the time that the application needs from its bootstrap until it finishes its main execution. The best way to do this is to define event listeners that are executed right after the "bootstrap" MVC event and right before the "finish" MVC event. The elapsed time will be printed to the standard error log. If you feel confident enough to perform this task all by yourself, then please proceed to do so in your favorite IDE, and come back only to compare solutions.

For those that prefer a step-by-step review, let's get started. The first file that we need to edit is the Module.php file for the Debug module. In it we have to add a listener that starts the time when the bootstrap event is triggered. We then need to add another listener that stops the time right before the finish event is triggered. The code changes that need to be applied to the onBootstrap method are the following:

```php
public function onBootstrap(MvcEvent $e)
    {
        $eventManager      = $e->getApplication()->getEventManager();
        $eventManager->attach('MvcEvent::EVENT_DISPATCH_ERROR', array($this, 'handleError'));
```

```
    // Below is how we get access to the service manager
    $serviceManager = $e->getApplication()->getServiceManager();
    // Here we start the timer
    $timer = $serviceManager->get('timer');
    $timer->start('mvc-execution');

    // And here we attach a listener to the finish event that has to be executed with priority 2
    // The priory here is 2 because listeners with that priority will be executed just before the
    // actual finish event is triggered.
    $eventManager->attach(MvcEvent::EVENT_FINISH, array($this,'getMvcDuration'),2);
}

public function getMvcDuration(MvcEvent $event)
{
    // Here we get the service manager
    $serviceManager = $event->getApplication()->getServiceManager();
    // Get the already created instance of our timer service
    $timer = $serviceManager->get('timer');
    $duration = $timer->stop('mvc-execution');
    // and finally print the duration
    error_log("MVC Duration:".$duration." seconds");
}
//...
```

If you add this code to your Module.php then you will see in the error log a line showing the time needed for the MVC part of the application to execute.

Notice that the code above works because the services by default are defined as shared. If this was not the case the result will be null.

Type the following to get the source code:

```
cd <full/path/to/>/learnzf2/
git stash
git checkout 'ch-service-time-calculation'
```

Best Practice

One of the most important things that we need to know when we work with services is to decide when to use them rather than just directly creating an instance of the class. If you look at the example above it may seem, at first glance, a bit over-engineered. But if we decide that this represents functionality helpful in other modules, which can be overwritten to provide improved functionality, then it starts to make more sense. Furthermore, when you use the service manager to retrieve instances of classes, the service manager does all the "heavy lifting" in trying to resolve, load, and instantiate the class.

Do not use anonymous functions for your services definition. If you missed the reason why then please read again the paragraph describing this in the discussion on Factories Definition.

If you now understand how the Event Manager and Service Manager work, then you have a firm foundation for understanding how the Model View Controller implementation works in ZF2.

Model View Controller

Model View Controller (MVC) is a design pattern that provides guidelines on how to structure your code so that you can more easily reuse it and separate the different concerns. Using MVC principles you write presentation logic into the view, application flow logic into the controller, and business logic into your model.

MVC Events

MVC workflow in ZF2 is controlled by events as summarized below:

Event Triggered	Notes
bootstrap	Signals the beginning of an application's MVC phase
route	The user request is matched to a controller and action
dispatch	The controller processes the application's logic flow
render	Any data which is to appear visually is rendered
finish	Signals that the MVC phase has completed

MVC Components

ZF2 implements a Model View Controller Architecture using a number of different components. In this section we will discuss some of the more common components.

Zend\Mvc\Router

Incoming request information is contained in a 'Request' object based on the Zend\Mvc\PhpEnvironment class. Zend\Mvc\Router is the ZF2 component which determines which module, controller and action to use. If the router finds a match in the routing table it returns a RouteMatch object.

In our ZF2 application we will describe the routes inside of the module configuration files only. It is possible to define them in other places within the module code as well, but we will refrain from doing so in order to improve readability and to avoid confusion.

There are different route types:

- Literal: "/contact"
- Segment: "/article/:id"
- Regex: "/tag/(?<tag>[^/]+)"
- Part/TreeRouteStack: tree of routes
- Wildcard: "/*"
- Hostname
- Scheme

TreeRouteStack Example
/blog -- Literal
  .xml -- Literal ("/blog.xml")
  /(?<id>[^/]+) -- Regex ("/blog/foo")
  /tag/(?<tag>[^/.]+) -- Regex ("/blog/tag/foo")
    .xml -- Literal ("/blog/tag/foo.xml")
  /year/:year -- Segment ("/blog/year/2011")
  /month/:year/:month -- Segment ("/blog/month/2011/12")

Zend\Mvc\Controller

Following the routing process, the matched action in the matched module and controller is called. In it we can process incoming application user data and save the processed data into a model or service.

In ZF2 the most basic controller is one which simply implements the Zend\Stdlib\Dispatch-ableInterface. The example below shows such a controller.

```php
<?php
namespace Foo\Controller;

use Zend\Stdlib\DispatchableInterface;
use Zend\Stdlib\RequestInterface;
use Zend\Stdlib\ResponseInterface;

class BasicController implements DispatchableInterface
{
  /* (non-PHPdoc)
   * @see \Zend\Stdlib\DispatchableInterface::dispatch()
   */
  public function dispatch(RequestInterface $request,ResponseInterface $response = null)
  {
    // TODO Auto-generated method stub
  }
}
```

In most cases you will not be dealing with basic controllers. Rather, you will be dealing more complex controllers such as the one shown below:

```php
<?php
namespace Foo\Controller;
use Zend\Mvc\Controller\AbstractActionController;

class CommonController extends AbstractActionController
{
  public function barAction()
  {
    // you get the incoming parameters from the request
    $request = $this->getRequest();
    $method  = $request->getMethod();
    $name = $this->getRequest()->getPost('name','DefaultName');

    // you can manipulate the response
    $response = $this->getResponse();
    if ($method == 'POST') {
      $response->setStatusCode('201');
    }

    // and you can pass information to the view just by returning it
    return array('name'=> $name);
  }
}
```

Zend\Mvc\Service

In some situations we might want to be more flexible and to provide the possibility of easily changing our model. In these cases, we can access our models indirectly via services that will provide us with the flexibility that we need. Our models should only contain business logic.

Zend\Mvc\View

The View component is used to visualize data passed from the controller. In ZF2 by default the view templates are PHP files, but you can also specify very easily other view types and mix them.

Model

The model in MVC can provide application data and includes business rules, logic, and functions. The model provides data and functionality that is grouped together for a common purpose. And there is more to be said: *"a model encapsulates more than just data and functions that operate on it. A model is meant to serve as a computational approximation or abstraction of some real world process or system. It captures not only the state of a process or system, but how the system works. This makes it very easy to use real-world modeling techniques in defining your models."*[18].

In ZF2 there is no Zend\Model superclass from which all models inherit. This is because *"the model is your business logic and it's up to you to decide how you want it to work"*[19]. Nevertheless ZF2 helps with the creation of some types of models. For the models that represent a database table there is the Zend\Db\TableGateway component. For the models that consume and publish information from RSS or Atom feeds there is the Zend\Feed component. Later in the book we will see how to use Zend\Db\TableGateway.

---

18 http://ootips.org/mvc-pattern.html
19 http://framework.zend.com/manual/2.2/en/user-guide/database-and-models.html

View

View Models

View models are containers for view variables, with some extra functionality. In the example below, once the controller action finishes execution, a view model will be created in the next stage.

```
class IndexController extends AbstractActionController
{
    public function indexAction()
    {
        //..
        return array(
                'version'=> $config['application']['version'],
                'applicationName' => $config['application']['name']
        );
    }
}
```

The view model variables will originate from the array returned by the index action. The created view model will be matched with a view template with a name based on the module, the controller and the action. In our case the view template name will be 'application/index/index'. When the time comes for rendering the view model a resolver will try to find an existing file that is mapped to template directory which matches the module name, a subdirectory which matches the controller, and a file which matches the action.

If we want to use different view template name in our action then we can do the following:

```
use Zend\View\Model\ViewModel;

class IndexController extends AbstractActionController
{
    public function indexAction()
    {
        // ...
        $viewModel = new ViewModel();
        $viewModel->setVariables(array(
                    'version'=> $config['application']['version'],
                'applicationName' => $config['application']['name']
            ));
        $viewModel->setTemplate('application/index/about');

        return $viewModel;
    }
}
```

Notice in this example that we directly return a view model, which instructs ZF2 to use this one, rather than constructing a default view model.

You can stack view models. One model can have multiple child view models. During the rendering process the child view models are rendered first, and then their content is used by the parent view model. Take a look at the following example:

```
public function indexAction()
{
        // layout will be our parent model
        $layoutViewModel = new ViewModel();
        // it must render view template with name 'layout/layout'
        $layoutViewModel->setTemplate('layout/layout');


        $viewModel = new ViewModel();
        $viewModel->setVariables(array(
                        'version'=> $config['application']['version'],
                        'applicationName' => $config['application']['name']
                ));
        $viewModel->setTemplate('application/index/about');

        // We add the view model as a child to the layout
        // The rendered content from the child model will be used
        // as value for the content variable
        $layoutViewModel->addChild($viewModel, 'content');

        return $layoutViewModel;
}
```

Using this technique, we can stack multiple views and render the layout, our final response. It is possible also to prevent adding children to a view model. You might want to visualize only the content of the action, for example, and disable the application layout (if any), as shown below:

```
    public function indexAction()
    {
        $viewModel = new ViewModel();
        $viewModel->setVariables(array(
                        'version'=> $config['application']['version'],
                        'applicationName' => $config['application']['name']
                ));
        $viewModel->setTemplate('application/index/about');
        $viewModel->setTerminal(true);

        return $viewModel;
    }
```

Template Resolvers

I mentioned earlier that there are resolvers that try to match a template name, like 'application/index/index' to a view template file. In ZF2 there are two resolvers that can be used out of the box. The first one is looking at a *template map* and trying to find if the template name is in the map. In the Application module.config.php we have this defined as:

```
'view_manager' => array(
  // ..
  'template_map' => array(
    'layout/layout'  => __DIR__ . '/../view/layout/layout.phtml',
    'application/index/index' => __DIR__ . '/../view/application/index/index.phtml',
    //..
  ),
```

Thus if we want to render the view template with a name 'layout/layout' then the file module/Application/view/layout/layout.phtml will be used.

The other way to resolve a template name is to use the template path stack definition. In it you define the list of view directories under which we can find view template files. The definition in the Application module configuration is the following:

```
'view_manager' => array(
  // ..
  'template_path_stack' => array(
    __DIR__ . '/../view',
  ),
),
```

As an example, take the template name "application/index/about". The template stack resolver will look in all directories specified, in the order defined, to see if there is a file that matches **<view-path>/application/index/about.phtml**.

Bear in mind that the resolver starts to look for the view template file first in the map and if no match is found it then uses the template path stack to look further.

Layout

The layout in ZF2 is implemented as a parent View model that has one child: the view model from the action. When the layout is ready to be rendered, the content from the controller action view model is added to the overall output. If the layout is not desired, in the view model section above we showed you how to disable the layout per action.

It is possible from an action to change the layout. For that you need to get the layout controller plugin and set the template to the new one, as show below:

```
class IndexController extends AbstractActionController
{
  public function indexAction()
  {
      $serviceLocator = $this->getServiceLocator();
      $config = $serviceLocator->get('config');

      $this->layout()->setTemplate('layout/embedded');

      return array(
              'version'=> $config['application']['version'],
              'applicationName' => $config['application']['name']
      );
  }
}
```

For our Debug module we want to add a new layout around the existing one, and to show debug information. One way will be to use the content of the already existing layout and create a new layout based on it. This solution is difficult to maintain, however, because with every change of the original layout you will have to change the debug layout as well. ZF2 allows us to solve that task in a very elegant way.

In the Debug Module.php we will attach a listener to the dispatch event:

```php
public function onBootstrap(MvcEvent $e)
{
    $eventManager = $e->getApplication()->getEventManager();
    $eventManager->attach('MvcEvent::EVENT_DISPATCH_ERROR', array($this, 'handleError'));

    // ...

    $eventManager->attach(MvcEvent::EVENT_RENDER,
            array($this,'addDebugOverlay'),
            100)
```

And the callback will add an overlay to the existing layout, without the need to know the original layout.

```php
<?php
namespace Debug;
//...
use Zend\View\Model\ViewModel;

class Debug
{
    //...
    public function addDebugOverlay(MvcEvent $event)
    {
        $viewModel = $event->getViewModel();

        $sidebarView = new ViewModel();
        $sidebarView->setTemplate('debug/layout/sidebar');
        $sidebarView->addChild($viewModel, 'content');

        $event->setViewModel($sidebarView);
    }
}
```

At that phase of the execution the MvcEvent object $event will give us access to the view model. The latter is the original layout view model. We will create a new view model and add the original layout as a child, setting the template to 'debug/layout/sidebar'. Finally, for all this to work, we need to set the view model to our new sidebar view model. The overlay layout is saved as module/Debug/view/debug/layout/sidebar.phtml and contains the following code:

```
<h1>Top Line</h1>
<?= $this->content ?>

<h1>Bottom Line</h1>
```

If you want to get the source code, enter these commands:

```
cd <full/path/to/>/learnzf2/
git stash
git checkout 'ch-view'
```

User Module

It is time to practise again, this time creating our second ZF2 module with the name User. Don't forget that automated wizards in IDEs like Zend Studio 10 can help you make this in seconds. After the module is created be sure to enable it in the application configuration file.

The goal of our User module will be to allow us to manage users as well as allowing them to log in and to log out. First we will start with the creation of the Account controller that will allow us to manage users. The controller file must be placed in the directory module/User/src/User/ Controller. The content of the Account controller at this stage is shown below:

```php
<?php
namespace User\Controller;

use Zend\Mvc\Controller\AbstractActionController;

class AccountController extends AbstractActionController
{
    public function indexAction()
    {
        return array();
    }

    public function addAction()
    {
        return array();
    }

    /*
    * Anonymous users can use this action to register new accounts
    */
    public function registerAction()
    {
        return array();
    }

    public function viewAction()
    {
        return array();
    }

    public function editAction()
    {
        return array();
    }

    public function deleteAction()
    {
        return array();
    }
}
```

Next, we have to describe our controller in the User module config file. Open it and add the following definition to the array returned:

```
'controllers' => array(
    'invokables' => array(
        // below is key               and below is the fully qualified class name
        'User\Controller\Account' => 'User\Controller\AccountController',
    ),
),
```

The definitions under the 'controllers' key of the array are quite similar to the definition of a service. Here we use the invokables definition. For the key User\Controller\Account we specify a class with the fully qualified name User\Controller\AccountController.

From your browser, if you were to enter http://localhost/user/account/add, you will get an error page saying "Unable to render template "user/account/add"; resolver could not resolve to a file". In this case the error indicates that we are missing a view template. We will have to create it as the file **module/User/view/user/account/add.phtml**. Please proceed to do so, and then reload the page in the web browser. You should see the web application now running successfully.

You may ask yourself how it was possible from the URL to indicate the "add" action in the Account controller. This was possible due to the already existing default route definition in your new User module. Open your module config file and look for a definition like the following:

```
'router' => array(
    'routes' => array(
        'user' => array(
            'type'   => 'Literal',
            'options' => array(
                // Change this to something specific to your module
                'route'   => '/user',
                'defaults' => array(
                    // Change this value to reflect the namespace in which
                    // the controllers for your module are found
                    '__NAMESPACE__' => 'User\Controller',
                    'controller'   => 'Account',
                    'action'       => 'index',
                ),
            ),
            'may_terminate' => true,
            'child_routes' => array(
                'default' => array(
                    'type'   => 'Segment',
                    'options' => array(
                        'route'   => '/[:controller[/:action]]',
                        'constraints' => array(
                            'controller' => '[a-zA-Z][a-zA-Z0-9_-]*',
                            'action'     => '[a-zA-Z][a-zA-Z0-9_-]*',
                        ),
                        'defaults' => array(
```

```
            ),
          ),
        ),
      ),
    ),
  ),
),
```

To get the source code for this example, type the following commands:

```
cd <full/path/to/>/learnzf2/
git stash
git checkout 'ch-account-controller'
```

Filters, Validators and Forms

Filtering

The Zend\Filter component contains ZF2 classes designed to sanitize the content of input data. You will be using it indirectly by building an InputFilter and adding Input elements to it. The code below describes how you can add filtering to an element, pass the data and retrieve the filtered data:

```php
<?php
use Zend\InputFilter\InputFilter;
use Zend\InputFilter\Input;

// This is how we create the element and add filtering rules to it
$phone = new Input();
$phone->getFilterChain()->attachByName('digits')
                ->attachByName('stringtrim');


// This is how we create the input filter and add the phone element to it
$filter = new InputFilter();
$filter->add($phone ,'phone');

$data = array (
    'phone' => '00123/4567-89',
);


// This is how we pass the raw data for filtering
$filter->setData($data);


// And this is how we get the filtered data
$phoneFilteredValue = $filter->getValue('phone');
```

In the example above we specified the filters by name. The names of the filters can be found by looking at the API documentation[20], or observing the files saved in the Zend\Filter directory inside the ZF2 source code. You will see files like Digits.php and StringTrim.php. These files contain code that does the actual filtering demonstrated in the example above.

Validating

Validating is the process of checking the value of an input against predefined rules. If the input does not match the rules, then the validation is considered unsuccessful. In the code above we can specify the set of allowed characters for phone numbers. The code below is an addition for the previous example and describes how to add a validator and check the validity of the data.

---

20 http://framework.zend.com/apidoc/2.1/namespaces/Zend.html

```php
<?php
use Zend\InputFilter\InputFilter;
use Zend\InputFilter\Input;
use Zend\Validator\Regex;

// This is how we create the element and add filtering rules to it
$phone = new Input();
$phone->getFilterChain()->attachByName('digits')
                ->attachByName('stringtrim');

// This is one of the ways to add a validator
$phone->getValidatorChain()->addValidator(new Regex('/^[\d-\/]+$/'));


// This is how we create the input filter and add the phone element to it
$filter = new InputFilter();
$filter->add($phone,'phone');

$data = array (
        'phone' => '00123 / 4567 - 89',
);

// This is how we pass the raw data for filtering
$filter->setData($data);

// This is how we validate the data
if($filter->isValid()) {
        // And this is how we get the filtered data
        $phoneFilteredValue = $filter->getValue('phone');
}
```

You can find the different available validators in the API documentation, or in the library code under Zend\Validator. Pay attention to the fact that data is first filtered, and then the filtered data is validated.

InputFilter Factory

In ZF2 it is possible to define the filters and validators in an array and pass this array to an In-putFilter Factory. Accordingly, the input filter definition above could be rewritten as follows:

```php
<?php
use Zend\InputFilter\Factory;

$factory = new Factory();
$filter = $factory->createInputFilter(array(
    'phone' => array (
      'name'=>'phone',
```

```
'filters' => array (
        array('digits'),
        array('stringtrim'),
    ),
    'validators' => array (
      array(
          'name'=>'regex',
          'options'=> array (
             'pattern' => '/^[\d-V]+$/',
          )
      ),
    )
  )
));

//..
```

Filtering and validating are among several components that ZF2 uses in conjunction with Zend\Form.

Forms

ZF2 provides a component that allows us to describe a HTML form, adding server side validation and filtering of user input. For our User module we will create a form that will be used for user management and save it with the filename module/User/src/Form/User.php. In this case our form will extend Zend\Form and will contain elements to be added later. The initial content of the form looks like this:

```php
<?php
namespace User\Form;

use Zend\Form\Form;

class User extends Form
{
        public function __construct()
        {
            parent::__construct();
        }
}
```

Elements

We can now add elements to the form. For a start we will collect user email addresses, which will be also be their login name. We will also need the following information: password, representative name, phone number and a picture. The code below shows how we add the email element to the form:

```php
<?php
namespace User\Form;

use Zend\Form\Form;

class User extends Form
{
    public function __construct()
    {
            parent::__construct();

    // This is how we define the "email" element
    $this->add(array(
        'name' => 'email', // the unique name of the element in the form.
                    //Ex: <input name="..."
        'type' => 'Zend\Form\Element\Email',
// The above must be valid Zend Form element.
// You can also use short names as "email" instead of "Zend\Form\Element\Email
        'options' => array(
            // This is list of options that we can add to the element.
            'label' => 'Email:'
            // Label is the text that should who before the form field
        ),
        'attributes' => array(
        // These are the attributes that are passed directly to the HTML element
            'type' => 'email', // Ex: <input type="email"
            'required' => true, // Ex: <input required="true"
            'placeholder' => 'Email Address...', // HTML5 placeholder attribute
        )
    ));


    }
}
```

The attributes array above allows us to set HTML attributes. HTML 5 in modern web browsers gives us client side data validation without extra JavaScript code by simply specifying special HTML 5 input attributes.

The phone element for example can be defined as follows:

```
$this->add(array(
    'name' => 'phone',
    'options' => array(
        'label' => 'Phone number'
    ),
    'attributes' => array(
        // Below: HTML5 way to specify that the input will be phone number
        'type' => 'tel',
        'required' => 'required',
        // Below: HTML5 way to specify the allowed characters
        'pattern'  => '^[\d-/]+$'
    ),
));
```

However this does not automatically add Zend validators to the form element. Therefore you will have to add them if you want to have server side data validation as well as client side HTML 5 validation.

Security Notice
You must never trust the incoming data. The verification of the input data on the browser is convenient for the user, but does not guarantee that the data will be filtered and validated as expected. This is due to the fact that the data may come also from a specially crafted HTTP request where an attacker is using input data to exploit potential security problems.

The final form definition looks like this:

```php
<?php
namespace User\Form;

use Zend\Form\Form;

class User extends Form
{
    public function __construct($name='user')
    {
        parent::__construct($name);

        $this->setAttribute('method', 'post');

        // This is how we define the "email" element
        $this->add(array(
            'name' => 'email', // the unique name of the element in the form.
                        //Ex: <input name="..."
            'type' => 'Zend\Form\Element\Email',
        // The above must be valid Zend Form element.
        // You can also use short names as "email" instead of "Zend\Form\Element\Email
            'options' => array(
```

```
    // This is list of options that we can add to the element.
    'label' => 'Email:'
    // Label is the text that should who before the form field
  ),
  'attributes' => array(
  // These are the attributes that are passed directly to the HTML element
    'type' => 'email', // Ex: <input type="email"
    'required' => true, // Ex: <input required="true"
    'placeholder' => 'Email Address...', // HTM5 placeholder attribute
  )
));


$this->add(array(
  'name' => 'password',
  'type' => 'Zend\Form\Element\Password',
  'attributes' => array(
    'placeholder' => 'Password Here...',
    'required' => 'required',
  ),
  'options' => array(
    'label' => 'Password',
  ),
));

$this->add(array(
  'name' => 'password_verify',
  'type' => 'Zend\Form\Element\Password',
  'attributes' => array(
    'placeholder' => 'Verify Password Here...',
    'required' => 'required',
  ),
  'options' => array(
    'label' => 'Verify Password',
  ),
));

$this->add(array(
    'name' => 'name',
    'type' => 'Zend\Form\Element\Text',
    'attributes' => array(
                    'placeholder' => 'Type name...',
                    'required' => 'required',
    ),
    'options' => array(
                    'label' => 'Name',
    ),
```

```php
));

$this->add(array(
    'name' => 'phone',
    'options' => array(
                    'label' => 'Phone number'
    ),
    'attributes' => array(
        // Below: HTML5 way to specify that the input will be phone number
                    'type' => 'tel',
                    'required' => 'required',
        // Below: HTML5 way to specify the allowed characters
                    'pattern'  => '^[\d-/]+$'
    ),
));

$this->add(array(
    'type' => 'Zend\Form\Element\File',
    'name' => 'photo',
    'options' => array(
      'label' => 'Your photo'
    ),
    'attributes' => array(
      'required' => 'required',
      'id'  => 'photo'
    ),
));

// This is the special code that protects our form beign submitted from automated scripts
$this->add(array(
  'name' => 'csrf',
  'type' => 'Zend\Form\Element\Csrf',
));

// This is the submit button
$this->add(array(
    'name' => 'submit',
    'type' => 'Zend\Form\Element\Submit',
    'attributes' => array(
                    'value' => 'Submit',
                    'required' => 'false',
    ),
));

    }

}
```

InputFilter

For every form we can define an input filter with filters and validators to match the different form elements. If you want to have the input filter declaration in the same class as the Form, you can add the *getInputFilter* method that can start as follows:

```php
<?php
namespace User\Form;

use Zend\Form\Form;
use Zend\InputFilter\InputFilter;
use Zend\InputFilter\InputFilterInterface;
use Zend\InputFilter\Factory as InputFactory;

class User extends Form
{
  //...
  public function getInputFilter()
  {
        if (! $this->filter) {
                $inputFilter = new InputFilter ();
                $factory = new InputFactory ();

                $inputFilter->add ( $factory->createInput ( array (
                        'name' => 'email',
                        'filters' => array (
                                        array (
                                                'name' => 'StripTags'
                                        ),
                                        array (
                                                'name' => 'StringTrim'
                                        )
                        ),
                        'validators' => array (
                                        array (
                                                'name' => 'EmailAddress',
                                                'options' => array (
                                                        'messages' => array (

'emailAddressInvalidFormat' => 'Email address format is not invalid'
                                                        )
                                                )
                                        ),
                                        array (
                                                'name' => 'NotEmpty',
                                                'options' => array (
                                                        'messages' => array (
```

```
                    'isEmpty' => 'Email address is required'

)
                                                                              )
                                                          )
                                          )
                        ) ) );
    //...
        $this->filter = $inputFilter;
        }
        return $this->filter;
}
```

For our specific needs we would like to to check the following on the server:
Is the email address valid?

```
$inputFilter->add ( $factory->createInput ( array (
                        'name' => 'email',
                        'filters' => array (
                                        array (
                                                        'name' => 'StripTags'
                                        ),
                                        array (
                                                        'name' => 'StringTrim'
                                        )
                        ),
                        'validators' => array (
                                        array (
                                                        'name' => 'EmailAddress',
                                                        'options' => array (

'messages' => array (

                        'emailAddressInvalidFormat' => 'Email address format is not invalid'
                                                                        )
                                                        )
                                        ),
                                        array (
                                                        'name' => 'NotEmpty',
                                                        'options' => array (
                                                                        'messages' => array (

                        'isEmpty' => 'Email address is required'
                                                                                        )
                                                                        )
                                                        )
                                        )
                        ) ) );
```

Verify the name and password are not empty

```
$inputFilter->add ( $factory->createInput ( array (
                        'name' => 'name',
                        'filters' => array (
                                array (
                                        'name' => 'StripTags'
                                ),
                                array (
                                        'name' => 'StringTrim'
                                )
                        ),
                        'validators' => array (
                                array (
                                        'name' => 'NotEmpty',
                                        'options' => array (
                                            'messages' => array (
                                                    'isEmpty' => 'Name is required'
                                            )
                                        )
                                )
                        )
                ) ) );
```

You have to provide a similar definition for the password element.

Verify the password is confirmed correctly

You might also want to add another password field in which the user is asked to repeat the password, in order to verify that the password is correct.

```
$inputFilter->add ( $factory->createInput ( array (
                        'name' => 'password_verify',
                        'filters' => array (
                                        array (
                                                'name' => 'StripTags'
                                        ),
                                        array (
                                                'name' => 'StringTrim'
                                        )
                        ),
                        'validators' => array (
                                        array (
                                                'name' => 'identical',
                                                'options' => array (
                                                            'token' => 'password'
                                                )
                                        )
                        )
                ) ) );
```

If the uploaded file is an image, we allow only png, gif and jpeg format.

Additionally we can specify file size limitation and image size limitation. The code below describes these requirements:

```
$inputFilter->add ( $factory->createInput ( array (
                'name' => 'photo',
                'validators' => array (
                        array (
                                'name' => 'filesize',
                                'options' => array (
                                        'max' => 2097152, // 2 MB
                                ),
                        ),
                        array (
                                'name' => 'filemimetype',
                                'options' => array (
                                        'mimeType' =>
                                'image/png,image/x-png,image/jpg,image/jpeg,image/gif',
                                )
                        ),
                        array (
                                'name' => 'fileimagesize',
                                'options' => array (
                                        'maxWidth' => 200,
                                        'maxHeight' => 200
                                )
                        ),
                )
)));
```

Additionally, for the file upload we can specify that the name of the uploaded file should be randomized and saved under data/image/photos/ (be sure to create this directory and make it writable by the web server). This can be done by adding a filter to the code above, as shown below:

```
        'name' => 'photo',
        'validators' => array (
//...
        ),
        'filters' => array (
                        // the filter below will save the uploaded file under
                        // <app-path>/data/images/photos/<tmp_name>_<random-data>
                        array (
                                'name'   => 'filerenameupload',
                                'options' => array (
        // Notice: Make sure that the folder below is existing on your system
        //          otherwise this filter will not pass and you will get strange
```

```
//          error message reporting that the required field is empty
                        'target'   => 'data/image/photos/',
                        'randomize' => true,
                    ),
                ),
            ),
//..
```

Does the phone number match the requirements?

For the phone validators and filter let us revisit the example used when we first started discussing InputFilter.

```
$inputFilter->add ( $factory->createInput ( array (
                'name' => 'phone',
                'filters' => array(
                        array ( 'name' => 'digits' ),
                        array ( 'name' => 'stringtrim' ),
                ),
                'validators' => array (
                        array (
                                'name' => 'regex',
                                'options' => array (
                                        'pattern' => '/^[\d-\/]+$/',
                                )
                        ),
                )
)));
```

Finalizing the input filter

If we want to prohibit changes to the form's new input filter just created, we will have to override the setInputFilter method with the following:

```
use Zend\InputFilter\InputFilterInterface;

// ..

public function setInputFilter(InputFilterInterface $inputFilter)
{
        throw new \Exception('It is not allowed to set the input filter');
}
```

Usage

From a controller, we can pass the defined form to the view for visualization and later on check the incoming data against it to see if it matches the specified rules. Our addAction in the User-Controller might look like this:

```php
<?php
namespace User\Controller;

use User\Form\User  as UserForm;

use Zend\Mvc\Controller\AbstractActionController;

class UserController extends AbstractActionController
{
//..
  public function addAction()
  {
    $form = new UserForm();
    if($this->getRequest()->isPost()) {
      $data = array_merge_recursive(
        $this->getRequest()->getPost()->toArray(),
        // Notice: make certain to merge the Files also to the post data
        $this->getRequest()->getFiles()->toArray()
      );
      $form->setData($data);
      if($form->isValid()) {
        // @todo: save the data of the new user
      }
    }

    // pass the data to the view for visualization
    return array('form1'=> $form);
  }
}
```

The post data will contain all post parameters except the file uploads. In order to get them from the request we have to use getFiles() as show in the highlighted lines above.

Display

Once the form is passed to the view we can display it using the built-in view helper formCollection. The initial version of the add.phtml view can be this:

```php
<?php
// We call the prepare here in order to fill the initial data and adjust the form properties,
// if needed
$this->form1->prepare();

echo $this->form()->openTag($this->form1);
// The helper below is the one that builds the form elements
echo $this->formCollection($this->form1);
echo $this->form()->closeTag();
?>
```

If we want to have tighter control over the form elements we can display them one by one as follows:

```
// visualizes the email element only
echo $this->formElement($this->form1->get('email'));
```

This will display the element without error messages, however. If you want to have the errors displayed as well, you can show them using the *formElementErrors* view plugin.

Below are changes made to improve the view (also incorporating the Bootstrap JavaScript library[21]):

```php
<?php
// We call the prepare here in order to fill the initial data and adjust the form properties, if needed
$this->form1->setAttribute('class','form-horizontal');
$this->form1->prepare();

echo $this->form()->openTag($this->form1);
echo '<fieldset>';

foreach($this->form1 as $element) {
        if(!($element instanceof Zend\Form\Element\Submit)) {
?>
  <div class="control-group">
                <label class="control-label" for="<?= $element->getName() ?>"><?= $this->translate($element->getLabel()) ?></label>
          <div class="controls">
      <?= $this->formElement($element) ?>
      <?= $this->formElementErrors($element)?>
          </div>
        </div>
<?php
        }
        else {
    $element->setAttribute('class', 'btn btn-primary');
?>
  <div class="form-actions">
<?=
    $this->formelement($element)
?>
  </div>
<?php

        }
}
```

---

21 http://twitter.github.com/bootstrap/

```
echo '</fieldset>';
echo $this->form()->closeTag();
?>
```

If you want to get the source code, enter the following:

```
cd <full/path/to/>/learnzf2/
git stash
git checkout 'ch-form'
```

We have now covered all of the basic information you will need to know in order to implement forms. Later in the book we have another chapter dealing with advanced form concepts such as custom form elements and their display. Be sure to read it if you want to become proficient in handling ZF2 forms.

Database

The database components from ZF2 allow us to communicate with different database engines and to perform operations on them.

Adapters

The adapters represent the actual connections to the database. For our application we will create a new service that instantiates the database object for us. We will save the file as **module/ User/src/User/Service/Factory/Database.php**. The content of the file will be this:

```php
<?php
namespace User\Service\Factory;

use Zend\ServiceManager\FactoryInterface;
use Zend\Db\Adapter\Adapter as DbAdapter;
use Zend\ServiceManager\ServiceLocatorInterface;

class Database implements FactoryInterface
{
        public function createService(ServiceLocatorInterface $serviceLocator)
        {
                $config = $serviceLocator->get('config');
                $adapter = new DbAdapter($config['db']);
                return $adapter;
        }
}
```

The recent versions of ZF2 include a ready-to-use database service factory called **Zend\Db\ Adapter\AdapterServiceFactory.**

When creating the database adapter instance probably the most important part is the db configuration. These parameters will vary across different installations and application environments. To account for this, in our module, we will create a new configuration file called **module/ User/config/database.local.php.dist** with the following content:

```php
<?php
return array (
    'db' => array(
        //The database driver. Mysqli, Sqlsrv, Pdo_Sqlite, Pdo_Mysql, Pdo=OtherPdoDriver
        'driver' => 'Mysqli',
        'database' => 'tc', // generally required the name of the database (schema)
        'username' => 'tc-db-username', // generally required the connection username
        'password' => 'tc-db-password', // generally required the connection password
        //not generally required the IP address or hostname to connect to
        'hostname' => 'localhost',
        // 'port' => 1234, // not generally required the port to connect to (if applicable)
        // 'charset' => 'utf8',  // not generally required the character set to use
        'options' => array (
```

```
        'buffer_results' => 1
    )
  )
);
```

In order to use the database configuration details you should copy this file to **config/autoload/database.local.php.** Notice that the *.dist* suffix is no longer in the name. You can now edit the copied file to match your current application environment.

Finally we need to describe our database adapter service in the service manager. This is nothing more than editing the *module/User/config/module.config.php* file and in the *service_manager* section adding the following:

```
'service_manager' => array (
    'factories' => array(
        'database' => 'User\Service\Factory\Database',
    )
),
```

The database object allows us to make queries to the database and additionally escape parameter values.

The following example demonstrates this

```
$db = $serviceLocator->get('database');
$db->query('SELECT id FROM users WHERE username=? AND password=?',
    array($login, $password)
    );
```

The **query** method, with certain exceptions (discussed below), generates prepared statements that can be executed. Data escaping is done automatically, using the correct escaping parameters. The developer need not be concerned about such details as the database adapter is aware of the requirements for the current database engine.

It is also possible to directly execute a statement without preparation. This is done by passing the constant **Zend\Db\Adapter\Adapter::QUERY_MODE_EXECUTE** as the second parameter of the query method call. In that case you have to take care to escape any data passed to the query in your code. Escaping the data can be done by retrieving the platform and from there calling one of its quote methods. In our case the code above can be changed to the following:

```
$escapedUsername = $db->getPlatform()->quoteValue($username);
$escapedPassword = $db->getPlatform()->quoteValue($password);
$sql = sprintf("SELECT id FROM users WHERE username='%s' AND password='%s",
               $escapedUsername, $escapedPassword);

$data = $db->query($sql, \Zend\Db\Adapter\Adapter::QUERY_MODE_EXECUTE);
```

The platform object gives us the access to the vendor specific SQL implementation details, including the way values are quoted (escaped), or the way identifiers are quoted.

Performance Notice

You have to be a bit careful when you use this method. If for example you might want to use it in a loop, such as in the following:

```
$pairs = array (
        // with 100 elements...
);
$db = $this->serviceManager->get('database');
foreach($pairs as $key=>$value) {
        $db->query('INSERT INTO properties(key,value) VALUES(?,?)',
        array($key, $value));
}
```

The code above will create 100 different prepared statements which will be executed. Creating a prepared statement has the disadvantage of taking more time and reserving resources. It makes much more sense to reuse the same prepared statement. In ZF2 we have the createStatement method which can be incorporated into the code to greatly improve performance as seen below:

```
$pairs = array (
   // with 100 elements...
);
$db = $this->serviceManager->get('database');
// 1. Prepare the statement once
$stmt = $db->createStatement('INSERT INTO properties(key,value) VALUES(?,?)');
foreach($pairs as $key=>$value) {
   // 2. Execute the statement
   $stmt->execute(array($key, $value));
}
```

Table Gateway

In our User module we want users to be able to perform base Create, Read, Update and Delete (CRUD) operations. We will now create a database table called "users" with the following syntax:

```
DROP TABLE IF EXISTS users;
CREATE TABLE users (
        id integer(11) auto_increment primary key,
        email varchar(255) NOT NULL unique,
        password varchar(80) NOT NULL,
        name varchar(255) NOT NULL,
        phone varchar(255),
        photo varchar(255),
        role varchar(50), -- we will store here the role of the user
        cdate datetime, -- created date
        mdate datetime -- modified date
);
```

This SQL statement can be saved into the file **module/User/sql/build.mysql.sql**. What you have to do now is to create the tc database and users table in your own MySQL installation. Once you are ready you can continue reading further about the Table Gateway [22].

The TableGateway component allows you to have an object representation of a table in the database. The code below is for creating a table gateway class that represents the users table. We will save the file as **module/Usr/src/User/Model/User.php**.

```php
<?php
namespace User\Model;

use Zend\Db\TableGateway\AbstractTableGateway;

class User extends AbstractTableGateway
{
        public function __construct()
        {
                $this->table = 'users';
        }
}
```

In order to use this model we need to pass the database adapter object to the constructor where we can assign the table name and adapter properties.

```php
class User extends AbstractTableGateway
{
        public function __construct($adapter)
        {
                $this->table = 'users';
                $this->adapter = $adapter;
        }
}
```

22 http://framework.zend.com/manual/2.1/en/modules/zend.db.table-gateway.html

If, in most cases, we use the same database adapter object, as is true at the moment for our User module, then we can improve our User model by changing the code as follows:

```php
<?php
namespace User\Model;

use Zend\Db\TableGateway\AbstractTableGateway;
use Zend\Db\TableGateway\Feature;

class User extends AbstractTableGateway
{
        public function __construct()
        {
                $this->table = 'users';
                $this->featureSet = new Feature\FeatureSet();
                $this->featureSet->addFeature(new Feature\GlobalAdapterFeature());
                $this->initialize();
        }
}
```

With the above changes our model will try to get the default database adapter object and use it. What is left is to add code in our module that sets the default database.

In our onBootstrap method we can add these lines at the end:

```php
public function onBootstrap($e)
{
   // existing code ...

   $services = $e->getApplication()->getServiceManager();
   $dbAdapter = $services->get('database');
   \Zend\Db\TableGateway\Feature\GlobalAdapterFeature::setStaticAdapter($dbAdapter);
}
```

The most important line (highlighted) sets the default database adapter.

The FeatureSet allows not only setting the default database adapter, but also adds advanced capabilities such as allowing separate reads and writes between different database adapters. The ZF2 documentation has a short explanation of the available features[23].

Now let's use the model in our controller to save the data supplied by the user. In the addAction method of the UserController, we can add the following code (highlighted):

```php
//..
use User\Model\User as UserModel;

//..
$form = new UserForm();
```

23 http://framework.zend.com/manual/2.1/en/modules/zend.db.table-gateway.html

```
if($this->getRequest()->isPost()) {
    //..
    if($form->isValid()) {
        // save the data of the new user
        $model = new UserModel();
        $id = $model->insert($form->getData());

        // @todo: redirect the user to the view user action
    }
}


return array('form'=> $form);//...
```

These few lines of code give us almost everything that we need to access the users table in the database. The form's getData method will return an array of key/value pairs.The names of the table columns will be taken from the keys, and the values will be the value portions of the array. Additionally, the model's insert method will ensure that the incoming data will be SQL escaped and safe for insertion.

You might have noticed that in the preceding paragraph I wrote "almost everything". As it stands right now, the photo and the password fields will need additional custom logic in order to be processed correctly. If we want to avoid copying and pasting this logic in other controllers, we will have to encapsulate it in the UserModel. We can override the UserModel's *insert* method with the following code:

```
public function insert($set)
{
        $set['photo'] = $set['photo']['tmp_name'];
        unset($set['password_verify']);
        $set['password'] = md5($set['password']); // better than clear text
                        //passwords
        return parent::insert($set);
}
```

Usability Notice

Unfortunately the needed changes just reviewed make things a bit ugly! Now our model code depends on the form definition, which in turn depends on the database structure, all of which is very fragile. If one of these components changes in the future version we will have to replicate the changes across the other components. In the advanced part of this book I will show you how this can be improved with the help of Doctrine 2.

The implementation of the deleteAction can look like this:

```
public function deleteAction()
{
    $id = $this->getRequest()->getQuery()->get('id');
    if($id) {
        $userModel = new UserModel();
        $userModel->delete(array('id'=> $id));
    }

    return array();
}
```

The delete method from the UserModel accepts a parameter of a different type. If you continue using an array to pass parameters, then ZF2 will ensure the id value is properly escaped and will help protect against SQL injection attacks.

TableGateway Service

Once I was asked: If we want to use the table gateway component, and have large number of tables in our database, do we have to create a class for every table? The answer is no. Generally we need a table gateway class for a table only if there is special logic that needs to be implemented. Otherwise, the database tables can be provided from a table gateway service that we will write next.

Create new factory service and save it as **module/User/src/User/Service/Invokable/Table-Gateway.php**. The initial version of the service can look like this:

```
<?php
namespace User\Service\Invokable;

use Zend\ServiceManager\ServiceLocatorAwareInterface;
use Zend\ServiceManager\ServiceLocatorInterface;
use Zend\Db\TableGateway\TableGateway as DbTableGateway;

class TableGateway implements ServiceLocatorAwareInterface
{
    /**
     * @var ServiceLocatorInterface
     */
    protected $serviceLocator;

    public function get($tableName, $features=null, $resultSetPrototype=null)
    {
        $db = $this->serviceLocator->get('database');

        $tableGateway = new DbTableGateway($tableName, $db, $features, $resultSetPrototype);
        return $tableGateway;
    }

    /* (non-PHPdoc)
     * @see \Zend\ServiceManager\ServiceLocatorAwareInterface::setServiceLocator()
```

```php
    */
    public function setServiceLocator(ServiceLocatorInterface $serviceLocator)
    {
            $this->serviceLocator = $serviceLocator;

    }

    /* (non-PHPdoc)
     * @see \Zend\ServiceManager\ServiceLocatorAwareInterface::getServiceLocator()
     */
    public function getServiceLocator()
    {
            $this->serviceLocator;
    }

}
```

For the cases where we already have existing table gateway class we will have to add additional checks.

```php
    public function get($tableName, $features=null, $resultSetPrototype=null)
    {
        $config  = $this->serviceLocator->get('config');
        // defined which class should be used for which table
        $tableGatewayMap = $config['table-gateway']['map'];
        if(isset($tableGatewayMap[$tableName])) {
            $className = $tableGatewayMap[$tableName];
            return new $className();
        }

        $db = $this->serviceLocator->get('database');
        $tableGateway = new DbTableGateway($tableName, $db, $features, $resultSetPrototype);
        return $tableGateway;
    }
```

And finally it makes sense to build a cache of instances, so we can add the following code to cache during the request.

```php
/**
 * @var array
 */
protected $cache;

    public function get($tableName, $features=null, $resultSetPrototype=null)
    {
        $cacheKey = $tableName;
        // $cacheKey = md5(serialize($tableName.$features.$resultSetPrototype));
```

```php
    if(isset($this->cache[$cacheKey])) {
        return $this->cache[$cacheKey];
    }

    $config  = $this->serviceLocator->get('config');
    // defined which class should be used for which table
    $tableGatewayMap = $config['table-gateway']['map'];
    if(isset($tableGatewayMap[$tableName])) {
        $className = $tableGatewayMap[$tableName];
        $this->cache[$cacheKey] = new $className();
    }
    else {
        $db = $this->serviceLocator->get('database');
        $this->cache[$cacheKey] = new DbTableGateway($tableName, $db, $features,
$resultSetPrototype);
    }

    return $this->cache[$cacheKey];
}
```

The module configuration table gateway map can look like this:

```php
'table-gateway' => array(
    'map' => array(
        'users' => 'User\Model\User',
    )
)
```

You can further improve the service and the configuration to specify when a table gateway object must use the master slave feature, or when to use special result set prototype.

If you want to get the source code for this section, run these commands.

```
cd <full/path/to/>/learnzf2/
git stash
git checkout 'ch-database-tablegateway'
```

Zend\Db\Sql

Ensuring that your SQL (Structured Query Language) statements still work when you change the database engine can be challenging. The reason for this is that most of the databases have their own variations from the standard SQL specification that make the query no longer executable when applied to a different database engine.

In ZF2 there is a component called Zend\Db\Sql that helps you write SQL statements that are reusable across different database platforms. All you have to do is to write an object oriented representation of SQL statement. The ZF2 reference manual [24] documentation for that component provides extensive information and here I will mention only briefly how we can use it for our application.

The following example will create an SQL select object that retrieves a list of users with id equal to 2.

---

24 http://framework.zend.com/manual/2.1/en/modules/zend.db.sql.html

```
use Zend\Db\Sql\Sql;

$sql = new Sql($adapter);
$select = $sql->select();
$select->from('users');
$select->where(array('id' => 2));
```

The *select* object is instance of $sql->select(). The tables from which the information will be fetched can be specified using the **from** method.

In the example above only one table is specified, but you can easily specify multiple tables by passing an array instead of a string.

```
$select->from(array('users','log'));
// = SELECT * FROM users, log WHERE id =2;
```

The key would represent the alias, and the value would represent the table name, as shown below:

```
$select->from(array('u'=>'users','l'=>'log'));
// = SELECT * FROM users u, log l WHERE id =2;
```

If you only want to fetch a subset of columns, you could use the columns method.

As with the from method, you can pass a string, describing a single column, or an indexed or associative array.

```
$select->columns(array('msg'=>'l.message', 'user'=> 'u.id'))->
from(array('u'=>'users','l'=>'log'));
// = SELECT l.message as msg, u.id as user FROM users u, log l WHERE id =2;
```

You can specify limits or offsets using the following syntax

```
$select->columns(array('msg'=>'l.message', 'user'=> 'u.id'))->
from(array('u'=>'users','l'=>'log'))->limit(10)->offset(0)
// = SELECT l.message as msg, u.id as user FROM users u, log l WHERE id =2 LIMIT 10 ;
```

If you want to sort the data you can use the *order* method.

```
$select->columns(array('msg'=>'l.message', 'user'=> 'u.id'))->
from(array('u'=>'users','l'=>'log'))->limit(10)->offset(0)
->order(array('id ASC'))
```

Once you have completed formulating the SQL object, you can prepare and execute it. The prepare–and-execute operation can be performed as given below:

```
$statement = $sql->prepareStatementForSqlObject($select);
$results = $statement->execute();
```

Otherwise, direct execution can be accomplished using the code below

```
$selectString = $sql->getSqlStringForSqlObject($select);
$results = $adapter->query($selectString, $adapter::QUERY_MODE_EXECUTE);
```

With the Zend\Db\Sql component you can write also insert, update and delete queries. The ZF2 reference manual has self explanatory examples you can check in order to master Zend\Db\Sql.

Database Profiling

In the latest version of ZF2 there is an already existing profiler that allows you to track what SQL queries were executed, their parameters and the time they needed to execute. For our application we will improve the Debug module and enable profiling for all database services. For that purpose, in the module.config.php file of the Debug module we will add the lines highlighted:

```
'service_manager' => array(
        'factories' => array(
                'timer' => 'Debug\Service\Factory\Timer',
        ),
        'initializers' => array(
                'Debug\Service\Initializer\DbProfiler',
        )
        ),
```

The service initializer will enable profiling for us. The code is saved as **module/Debug/src/Debug/Service/Initiliazer/DbProfiler.php** and has the following content:

```php
<?php
namespace Debug\Service\Initializer;

use Zend\ServiceManager\InitializerInterface;
use Zend\Db\Adapter\Profiler\Profiler;
use Zend\Db\Adapter\Profiler\ProfilerAwareInterface;
use Zend\ServiceManager\ServiceLocatorInterface;

class DbProfiler implements InitializerInterface
{
    /**
     *
     * @var Zend\Db\Adapter\Profiler\Profiler
     */
    protected $profiler;

    /**
     * Initialize
     *
     * @param $instance
     * @param ServiceLocatorInterface $serviceLocator
```

```php
 * @return mixed
 */
public function initialize($instance, ServiceLocatorInterface $serviceLocator)
{
    if ($instance instanceof ProfilerAwareInterface) {
        $instance->setProfiler($this->getProfiler($serviceLocator));
    }
}

public function getProfiler($serviceLocator)
{
    if(!$this->profiler) {
        if($serviceLocator->has('database-profiler')) {
            $this->profiler = $serviceLocator->get('database-profiler');
        } else {
            $this->profiler = new Profiler();
            $serviceLocator->setService('database-profiler', $this->profiler);
        }
    }
    return $this->profiler;
}
}
```

The most important lines are highlighted. In the *initialize()* method we check if the argument supplised as the first parameter is an instance of Zend\Db\Profiler\ProfilerAwareInterface, and if so, we inject the profiler object.

This is all that is needed to enable the profiler. Now, in order to show profiling results, having injected the profiler object, in the debug layout we can present the results. To have the injection take place we add the following to the Module.php file of the Debug module:

```php
class Module implements AutoloaderProviderInterface
{
    // ...
    public function onBootstrap(MvcEvent $e)
    {
        //..
        $eventManager->attach(MvcEvent::EVENT_RENDER,
                array($this,'injectViewVariables'),
                100);
        //...
    }

    /**
     * Injects common variables in the view model
     * @param MvcEvent $event
     */
    public function injectViewVariables(MvcEvent $event)
    {
```

```php
    $viewModel = $event->getViewModel();

    $services = $event->getApplication()->getServiceManager();
    $variables = array();
    if($services->has('database-profiler')) {
        // If we have database profiler service then we inject it in the view
        $profiler = $services->get('database-profiler');
        $variables['profiler'] = $profiler;
    }
    if(!empty($variables)) {
        $viewModel->setVariables($variables);
    }
  }
  // ...
}
```

And the debug layout (stored as module/Debug/view/debug/layout/sidebar.phtml) is as follows:

```php
<h1>Top Line</h1>
<?= $this->content ?>

<h1>Bottom Line</h1>
<?php
if ($this->profiler) {
        echo '<div id="profiler">Db Profiler:';
        foreach($this->profiler->getProfiles() as $profile) {
                echo ''. $profile['sql'].' ('.implode(',',
            $profile['parameters']->getNamedArray()).')" took '.
            $profile['elapse'].' seconds<br>';
        }
        echo '</div>';
}
?>
```

For situations where the output does not contain profiler information, but where SQL queries have been performed, we can add extra code that logs this information to the standard error output. In the Debug Module.php add the following:

```php
public function onBootstrap(MvcEvent $e)
{
  // ..
  $eventManager->attach(MvcEvent::EVENT_FINISH, array($this,'dbProfilerStats'),2);
}


public function dbProfilerStats(MvcEvent $event)
{
```

```
$services = $event->getApplication()->getServiceManager();
if($services->has('database-profiler')) {
    $profiler = $services->get('database-profiler');
    foreach ($profiler->getProfiles() as $profile) {
       $message = "" . $profile['sql'].' ('.implode(',',$profile['parameters']->getNamedArray()).')"
took '.$profile['elapse'].' seconds'."\n";
       error_log($message);
    }
  }
 }
}
```

If you want to get the source code, run these commands:

```
cd <full/path/to/>/learnzf2/
git stash
git checkout 'ch-database'
```

Routing

Routing is the process of mapping the incoming URL to a controller. A module that does not have controllers does not need to have a route map.

Describing a Route

The routing map is described in **module.config.php**. You must use the router key and under it use the routes key to describe the available routes. The definition below maps the URI "/" to a *router => [routes] key called home.*

```
'router' => array(
    'routes' => array(
        'home' => array(
            'type' => 'Zend\Mvc\Router\Http\Literal',
            'options' => array(
                'route'   => '/',
                'defaults' => array(
                    'controller' => 'Application\Controller\Index',
                    'action'   => 'index',
                ),
            ),
        ),
//...
),
//..
```

When you define a route you need to give it a name. The route defined in the code above is called home. For this route, and for every other route, we need to define the subkeys type and options. In the case above the type is 'Zend\Mvc\Router\Http\Literal'. The **"options"** defined above indicate that the controller with fully qualified name **"Application\Controller\Index"** and the action **"index"** must be used if the "/" route is matched.

For our User module we have the following routing definition:

```
'router' => array(
    'routes' => array(
        'user' => array(
            'type'   => 'Literal',
            'options' => array(
                // Change this to something specific to your module
                'route'   => '/user',
                'defaults' => array(
                    // Change this value to reflect the namespace in which
                    // the controllers for your module are found
                    '__NAMESPACE__' => 'User\Controller',
                    'controller'   => 'Account',
                    'action'     => 'me',
                ),
```

```
),
// … the children definition is coming…
```

It says that if somebody entered a URI /user then the controller **User\Controller\Account** and the action **index** must be used.

During the definition of a route you can also describe children of this route:

```
'may_terminate' => true,
'child_routes' => array(
    // This route is a sane default when developing a module;
    // as you solidify the routes for your module, however,
    // you may want to remove it and replace it with more
    // specific routes.
    'default' => array(
        'type'   => 'Segment',
        'options' => array(
            'route'   => '/[:controller[/:action]]',
            'constraints' => array(
                'controller' => '[a-zA-Z][a-zA-Z0-9_-]*',
                'action'    => '[a-zA-Z][a-zA-Z0-9_-]*',
            ),
            'defaults' => array(
            ),
        ),
    ),
),
```

If you enter URI matching the format '/user/[:controller[/:action]]', for example **/user/account/register**, then **account** will become the controller parameter, and **register** will be the action. The constraints option is used to define valid characters for controller and action.

You might want to obtain a parameter from routing. The route definition needed to obtain the id parameter is shown below:

```
'router' => array(
    'routes' => array(
        'user' => array(
            'type'   => 'Literal',
            'options' => array(
                // Change this to something specific to your module
                'route'   => '/user',
                'defaults' => array(
                    // Change this value to reflect the namespace in which
                    // the controllers for your module are found
                    '__NAMESPACE__' => 'User\Controller',
                    'controller'   => 'Account',
                    'action'      => 'me',
                ),
```

```
        ),
        'may_terminate' => true,
        'child_routes' => array(
            // This route is a sane default when developing a module;
            // as you solidify the routes for your module, however,
            // you may want to remove it and replace it with more
            // specific routes.
            'default' => array(
                'type'    => 'Segment',
                'options' => array(
                    'route'   => '/[:controller[/:action[/:id]]]',
                    'constraints' => array(
                        'controller' => '[a-zA-Z][a-zA-Z0-9_-]*',
                        'action'     => '[a-zA-Z][a-zA-Z0-9_-]*',
                        'id'         => '[0-9]*',
                    ),
                    'defaults' => array(
                    ),
                ),
            ),
        ),
    ),
),
```

Matched Route

During a request, once the routing process has completed, we call up the matched route definition, and can extract any parameters from it. In the Module.php file of the User module we can
attach an event listener that is executed after routing.

```
public function onBootstrap(MvcEvent $event)
{
    $services = $event->getApplication()->getServiceManager();
    //...
    $eventManager = $event->getApplication()->getEventManager();
    $eventManager->attach(MvcEvent::EVENT_ROUTE,
                array($this, 'protectPage'), -100);
    //...
}
```

In the callback, you can use the RouteMatch object returned from the *getRouteMatch()* method
to get the name of the controller, action, and other parameters.

```
public function protectPage(MvcEvent $event)
{
    $match = $event->getRouteMatch();
```

```
    if(!$match) {
            // we cannot do anything without a resolved route
            return;
    }

    $controller = $match->getParam('controller');
    $action    = $match->getParam('action');
    $namespace  = $match->getParam('__NAMESPACE__');
    //..
}
```

Using routes in controllers and views is simplified with the help of controller plugins and view plugins. The latter will be discussed in more detail in a later chapter.

Using Routes in Controller

Getting Route Parameters

You can use the params controller plugin to retrieve routing parameters. For example, in the Account controller, if you want to know which id was passed in the URI, you can write:

```
public function deleteAction()
{
    $id = $this->params()->fromRoute('id');
```

Redirecting to Route

Route definitions can also be used to redirect the browser to a new URL. The advantage to using the route definition is that the final URL is created correctly according to the current application, and will not be changed if you change the base URI, host, or other parameters of the URL. Below is an example:

```
public function deleteAction()
{
    $id = $this->params('id');
    if(!$id) {
        return $this->redirect()->toRoute('user/default', array(
            'controller' => 'account',
            'action' => 'view',
        ));
    }
```

The route that is used above is default, which is a child route of user. Notice that default and user are the names of the routes, not their URIs. And we pass parameters with the names controller and action, with values "account" and "view".

Using Routes in View

The route definition can be used to create valid URLs in the view portion of your application, using the url view plugin. In our Application module, the view/layout/layout.phtml view template contains the following code:

```
<a class="brand" href="<?php echo $this->url('home') ?>">
```

The result of the code above will be valid URL using the home route.

```
<a class="brand" href="/">
```

The use of the url view plugin guarantees that if you make changes to the routing definition the generated URL will still point to the correct place.

The url view plugin accepts a second parameter which can define options that you wish to pass.

```
<a href="<?php

echo $this->url('user/default', array(
            'controller'=>'log',
            'action'   => 'in',
        ));

?>">
```

This code will generate the URI using the route user, and its child route default, also including the controller and action parameters.

If you want to get the source code, run these commands:

```
cd <full/path/to/>/learnzf2/
git stash
git checkout 'ch-routing'
```

Plugins

Controller Plugins

Controller plugins provide additional functionality in the controller and simplify tasks such as getting parameters from a request, redirection or passing messages to the next request.

Redirect

This plugin helps us redirect the request to a new URL. It sets the Location header which instructs the browser to make a new request to the indicated URL.

As an example, from our Account controller in the User module, we would like to redirect after a successful addition. This can be achieved with the following code:

```
public function addAction()
{
  $form = new UserForm();
  if($this->getRequest()->isPost()) {
    // ...
    if($form->isValid()) {
      //...

      // redirect the user to the view user action
      return $this->redirect()->toRoute('user/default', array (
                  'controller' => 'account',
                  'action'    => 'view',
                  'id'   => $id
              ));
    }
  }

  // pass the data to the view for visualization
  return array('form1'=> $form);
}
```

Notice the **return** statement. If you do not return the value from the redirect plugin, it will continue to process the next calls in the method and will not redirect the browser properly. Also notice that the URL in the browser navigation bar will change to the redirected URL. For the purposes of redirection we used a route description.

Forward

This plugin allows us to make an internal redirect, within our application's current request cycle, instead of asking the browser to do this and generating a new browser request. In the User module, we modified the register action of the Account controller to perform a forward as follows:

```
/*
 * Anonymous users can use this action to register new accounts
 */
public function registerAction()
{
    $result = $this->forward()->dispatch('User\Controller\Account', array(
        'action' => 'add',
    ));

    return $result;
}
```

The dispatch method called from the forward plugin requires the fully qualified name of the controller. As a second argument you can pass parameters, such as the action, as shown in the example above. The dispatch will trigger a new dispatch event and all of your dispatch listeners will be re-executed. The URL in the browser will not change. As with the redirect plugin you will have to prefix the statement with return if you want to stop further execution of code in the same action.

Params

The next examples require you to fetch the skeleton Log controller. Execute the following commands to do this:

```
cd <full/path/to/>/learnzf2/
git stash
git checkout 'skeleton-log-controller'
```

The params plugin provides easy access to parameters coming from the request. These include both GET and POST parameters, headers and routing. To retrieve a parameter id, for example, regardless of the actual source of the incoming data (i.e. routing, GET, POST, etc.) you can use the following code in your controller:

```
$id = $this->params('id');
```

As an example, in the LogController::inAction() we wish to ensure that data is coming only from the post parameters. For this we can use the following code:

```
public function inAction()
{
    if (!$this->getRequest()->isPost())
    {
        // just show the login form
        return array();
    }

    $username = $this->params()->fromPost('username');
    $password = $this->params()->fromPost('password');
    // ...
```

FlashMessenger

The flash messenger plugin allows us to pass one or more messages to the next request. To add a message from a controller you can write the following:

```
$this->flashmessenger()->addMessage('You are now logged in.')
```

In our Log controller we would like to add a success message when the user is logged in, and an error message in case of failure. For the success message we can use this code:

```
public function inAction()
{
    if (!$this->getRequest()->isPost())
    {
        // just show the login form
        return array();
    }

    $username = $this->params()->fromPost('username');
    $password = $this->params()->fromPost('password');

    // @todo: When the authentication is implemented the hard-coded
    // value below has to be removed.
    $isValid = 1;
    if($isValid) {
        $this->flashmessenger()->addSuccessMessage('You are now logged in.');

        return $this->redirect()->toRoute('user/default', array (
                        'controller' => 'account',
                        'action'    => 'me',
        ));
    }
    else {
        // @todo: report some errors
    }

}
```

For adding an error message we can replace the *addSuccessMessage* method with the *addErrorMessage* method.

View Plugins

View plugins add additional functionality to our view, as do controller plugins for controllers.

Translate

Translate is a plugin that helps us translate text in the current language. We have already used this plugin in the Application module. In our User module we will use this feature in the view template **view/user/account/me.phtml**. The content of this view template is as follows:

```php
<?php
echo $this->translate('Your account');
```

Url

Url is a plugin that helps us create valid internet links for our application.This plugin makes our life easier in that it takes care of base path changes, changes in routes, and so forth. In the view template **view/user/account/denied.phtml** we see the following code:

```php
<?= $this->translate('You do not have access to this page.') ?>
<a href="<?php

echo $this->url('user/default', array(
                'controller'=>'log',
                'action'   => 'in',
            ));

?>"><?= $this->translate('Log in') ?></a> with user that has the correct access.
```

The *url* plugin above uses the route **"default"**, a child of the user route, and passes controller and action parameters.

FlashMessenger

The *flashmessenger* view plugin helps us to display messages across requests. As an example, we will change the application layout, and add code that shows the different type of messages. Our layout view has now the following code:

```php
<body>
    <div class="navbar navbar-inverse navbar-fixed-top">
    <!-- Menu Navigation ... -->
    </div>


<?php
  $namespaces = array ('error','success','info','default');
  foreach ($namespaces as $namespace) {
        $flashMessages = $this->flashmessenger()->render($namespace);
        if (!empty($flashMessages)) {
        ?>
<div id="myAlert" class="alert alert-<?= $namespace ?>" data-alert="alert">
    <a class="close" data-dismiss="alert">×</a>
    <?= $flashMessages ?>
</div>
<?php
    }
```

```
    }
?>
```

```
        <div class="container">
```

Now we can log in again and see if there is a nice green message on the screen telling us that we have logged in successfully.

If you want to get the source code type these commands:

```
cd <full/path/to/>/learnzf2/
git stash
git checkout 'skeleton-log-controller'
```

Better Code Quality

Unit Tests

In the next chapter we will be substantially refactoring our code. We will try to make it easier to maintain and less error prone. Before we start the refactoring process, however, we need to provide an infrastructure that can prove our code is still running. For this purpose we will show you how to write php unit tests for ZF2 code you will develop.

Installing PHPUnit

Because PHPUnit is important for the development, but not the running, of an application, we should add the following specification to the application composer.json file:

```
// ...
"require": {
    "php": ">=5.3.3",
    "zendframework/zendframework": "2.*",
    "doctrine/common": ">=2.1",
    "doctrine/orm": ">=2.1"
},
"require-dev": {
        "phpunit/phpunit" : "3.7.*"
}
}
```

And then, to have PHPUnit installed, we can run composer with the following command:

```
php composer.phar install --dev
```

The *--dev* flag instructs *composer* to install the development requirements. Without this flag only the application requirements will be downloaded.

Running PHPUnit

Our main focus is the User module. As it was created using Zend Studio 10, a tests directory is also created with all needed files in place for our first test. Go to the main application directory:

```
php composer.phar install --dev
```

And then run phpunit:

```
ZF2_PATH=`pwd`/vendor/zendframework/zendframework/library \
php vendor/bin/phpunit -c module/User/tests/
```

The result should be something like this:

PHPUnit 3.7.18 by Sebastian Bergmann.

Configuration read from <full/path/to/>/learnzf2/module/User/tests/phpunit.xml

Time: 0 seconds, Memory: 4.00Mb

OK (1 test, 1 assertion)

Writing Tests

Before we start writing tests we need to check a few details. Our phpunit.xml file in the module/User/tests directory should look like this:

```
<phpunit bootstrap="./bootstrap.php" colors="true">
<testsuites>
  <testsuite name="User Test Suite">
    <directory>./</directory>
  </testsuite>
</testsuites>
</phpunit>
```

There should be User and config directories under module/Users/tests. In the config directory there should be an application.config.php file. This file contains the test application configuration and looks like this:

```php
<?php
return array(
  'modules' => array(
    'Application',
    'User',
  ),
  'module_listener_options' => array(
    'config_glob_paths'   => array(
      // Below are the actual configuration files for the application
      'config/autoload/{,*.}{global,local}.php',
      // Here are overrides for the test itself
      __DIR__.'/test/{,*.}{global,local}.php',
    ),
    'module_paths' => array(
      'module',
      'vendor',
    ),
  ),
);
```

In the test application configuration I enabled the User module and the Application module. The latter one is enabled because our User module depends on it to have a working application. If there were other modules on which our User module was dependant, then they should have been enabled too. Other modules should not be enabled in this test application configuration.

Notice that in the configuration file I specified the following:

```
'config_glob_paths'  => array(
      // Below are the actual configuration files for the application
      'config/autoload/{,*.}{global,local}.php',
      // Here are overrides for the test itself
      __DIR__.'/test/{,*.}{global,local}.php',
    ),
```

The highlighted code above means that my test configuration will load the actual application global and local files first. But if I want to have some specific settings for the test environment I should add them in the **module/User/tests/config/test/** directory. For example if I decide to use another database configuration for the test, I could store it in a file **module/User/tests/config/test/database.local.php.**

Testing controllers

Once we are ready with the setup, we can write our first controller test, which will test the Account controller. The initial version of the test file must be saved under **module/User/tests/UserTest/Controller/AccountControllerTest.php** and has the following content.

```
<?php
namespace UserTest\Controller;

use Zend\Test\PHPUnit\Controller\AbstractHttpControllerTestCase;

class AccountControllerTest extends AbstractHttpControllerTestCase
{
  protected $traceError = true;

  public function setUp()
  {
        $this->setApplicationConfig(
                        include __DIR__.'/../../config/application.config.php'
        );
        parent::setUp();
  }
}
```

It is important for our tests to extend from *AbstractHttpControllerTestCase*, which is under the Zend\Test component family. If we want to see more information in case of an error, the *$traceError* attribute should be set to true. Finally, the setup method must load the application configuration that is stored in the **tests/config** directory.

The first test will be for the "me" action. We will check to see if dispatching the URL "/user/account/me" brings us to the controller **User\Controller\Account**:

```
  public function testMeAction()
  {
        $this->dispatch('/user/account/me');
```

```
        $this->assertActionName('me');
        $this->assertControllerName('User\Controller\Account');
    }
```

Now run the test as follows:

```
cd <full/path/to/>/learnzf2/
ZF2_PATH=`pwd`/vendor/zendframework/zendframework/library \
php vendor/bin/phpunit -c module/User/tests/
```

On my machine the test failed with a strange error saying "Illegal Offset", pointing to the *translate* service. The reason for this is that PHPUnit by default treats warnings as errors. I have two choices to fix the problem: translate all strings that are in the view, or something better: instruct PHPUnit during the initial development to stop treating the warnings as errors.

```
<phpunit bootstrap="./bootstrap.php" colors="true" convertWarningsToExceptions="false">
  <testsuites>
    <testsuite name="User Test Suite">
      <directory>./</directory>
    </testsuite>
  </testsuites>
</phpunit>
```

Now run the test again and see if everything works as expected.

Inside our unit tests we can gain access to the application object, and from there access to the service and event managers.

```
public function testMeAction()
{
        $application = $this->getApplication();
        $serviceManager = $application->getServiceManager();
        $eventManager  = $application->getEventManager();

        $this->dispatch('/user/account/me');

        $this->assertActionName('me');
        $this->assertControllerName('User\Controller\Account');
}
```

Later in this book we will use these managers to improve our tests.

Notice

The dispatch method from the test case simulates a user launching a request from a browser. It accepts a url as a first argument, an HTTP method as a second one, and parameters as third.

In order to control the input and the output from a dispatch, we can use the request, response and result objects as shown below:

```php
public function testMeAction()
{
        $application = $this->getApplication();
        $serviceManager = $application->getServiceManager();
        $eventManager  = $application->getEventManager();

        // This is how the request object can be accessed and modified.
        $request = $this->getRequest();

        // The dispatch method returns the result.
        $result = $this->dispatch('/user/account/me');


        $this->assertActionName('me');
        $this->assertControllerName('User\Controller\Account');

        // This is how the response object can be accessed.
        $response = $this->getResponse();

        // And here we can use the response to check the status code.
        $this->assertEquals(200, $response->getStatusCode());
}
```

If you want to get the source code, run these commands:

```
cd <full/path/to/>/learnzf2/
git stash
git checkout 'ch-unittest'
```

Coding Styles

Coding styles are rules which suggest how to properly format your code. Adhering to these rules makes the code base more consistent, easy to read and to maintain. They improve the overall quality of our application in that any developer reviewing the code knows what to expect.

From this point we will start adhering to the ZF2 coding styles in our application and modules. ZF2 uses the PSR-225 standard. I will show you how to fix the code automatically that we have developed so far, and also how to ensure that future changes to the code do not break the coding style.

First download in the main application directory a PHP tool called *php-cs-fixer* [26].

```
cd <full/path/to/>/learnzf2/
wget http://cs.sensiolabs.org/get/php-cs-fixer.phar
```

---

25 https://github.com/php-fig/fig-standards/blob/master/accepted/PSR-2-coding-style-guide.md
26 http://cs.sensiolabs.org/

Once the application is downloaded we can run it to check the existing modules. If we want only to report information, without actually fixing anything we can use the following commands:

```
cd <full/path/to/>/learnzf2/
php php-cs-fixer.phar fix -v --dry-run --level=psr2 module/
```

In order to apply the automatic changes you have to remove the –dry-run parameter. I will demonstrate fixing the code for the module/ and config/ directories only, as these are the directories that contain PHP code we directly wrote.

```
cd <full/path/to/>/learnzf2/
php php-cs-fixer.phar fix -v --level=psr2 module/
php php-cs-fixer.phar fix -v --level=psr2 config/
```

If you are interested to see what has changed, you can use git to display the differences:

```
cd <full/path/to/>/learnzf2/
git diff
```

If we want to maintain our own coding style, we can periodically run php-cs-fixer manually, or we can automate this process. My colleague Enrico Zimuel gave me a hint that a git pre-commit hook already exists which the ZF2 team is using27, so I decided to use it with small modifications to fit our purposes. It reports problems and prevents the code from being committed, but at the same time it also fixes the code automatically. Using this technique, we, as developers, can see any changes and have the final word.

```php
#!/usr/bin/env php
<?php
/**
 * .git/hooks/pre-commit
 *
 * This pre-commit hooks will check for PHP errors (lint), and make sure the
 * code is PSR-2 compliant.
 *
 * Dependecy: PHP-CS-Fixer (https://github.com/fabpot/PHP-CS-Fixer)
 *
 * @author  Mardix  http://github.com/mardix
 * @author  Matthew Weier O'Phinney http://mwop.net/
 * @since   4 Sept 2012
 */

$exit = 0;

/*
 * collect all files which have been added, copied or
 * modified and store them in an array called output
 */
$output = array();
```

---

27 https://github.com/zendframework/zf2/blob/master/README-GIT.md

```php
exec('git diff --cached --name-status --diff-filter=ACM', $output);

foreach ($output as $file) {
  if ('D' === substr($file, 0, 1)) {
    // deleted file; do nothing
    continue;
  }

  $fileName = trim(substr($file, 1));

  /*
   * Only PHP files
   */
  if (!preg_match('/\.ph(p|tml)(\.dist){0,1}$/', $fileName)) {
    continue;
  }

  /*
   * Check for parse errors
   */
  $output = array();
  $return = 0;
  exec("php -l " . escapeshellarg($fileName), $output, $return);

  if ($return != 0) {
    echo "PHP file fails to parse: " . $fileName . ":" . PHP_EOL;
    echo implode(PHP_EOL, $output) . PHP_EOL;
    $exit = 1;
    continue;
  }

  /*
   * PHP-CS-Fixer
   */
  $dryRun='';
  $output = array();
  $return = null;
  exec("git config --get phpcs.dry", $output, $return);
  if (!empty($output[0])) {
    $dryRun='--dry-run';
  }
  $cwd = '';
  $gitDir = $_SERVER['GIT_DIR'];
  if ($gitDir != '.git') {
    $cwd = dirname($gitDir);
  }
  if ($cwd == '') {
```

```php
    $cwd = '.';
  }

  $output = array();
  $return = null;
      exec("$cwd/php-cs-fixer.phar fix -v $dryRun --level=psr2 " . escapeshellarg($fileName),
$output, $return);
  $errors = array();
  for($i=0; $i<count($output); $i++) {
    if($output[$i][0]=='!') {
      continue;
    }
    $errors[]=$output[$i];
  }
  if ($return != 0 || !empty($errors)) {
    echo "PHP file contains CS issues: " . $fileName . ":" . PHP_EOL;
    echo implode(PHP_EOL, $errors) . PHP_EOL;
    $exit = 1;
    continue;
  }
}

if($exit) {
    print "Aborting commit! Run\n\tgit diff\nto see the code with fixed coding style. ".
        "Take a look at the changed file(s) and if you like the correction(s) run".
        "\n\tgit add <changed-file>\n".
        "And try to commit the changes again.\n";
}

exit($exit);
```

If you want to use this script as a hook make sure that you have saved it as .git/hook/pre-commit and that the file is executable.

Finally, run the unit tests to make sure that everything is working as before.

Better Reusability

Hydrators

"Hydration is the act of populating an object from a set of data. The Hydrator is a simple component to provide mechanisms both for hydrating objects, as well as extracting data sets from them."[28]

Hydrators define how the data must be passed to the object (hydration) and how to read data from it (extraction). At the time of this writing, in ZF2, there are four hydrator implementations. I will now go through them and provide brief explanations.

Zend\Stdlib\Hydrator\ArraySerializable

This hydrator is useful for objects that extend ArrayObject. Target objects must implement either the exchangeArray() or the populate() method to support hydration, and the getArrayCopy() method to support extraction.

Zend\Stdlib\Hydrator\ClassMethods

Any class that has getter and setter methods for its properties can use this hydrator. Setter methods will be called in order to hydrate, and getter methods will be called for extraction.

Zend\Stdlib\Hydrator\ObjectProperty

Any class that has public properties can use this hydrator. The data is taken directly from the property and no setter or getter methods are called. This makes the hydration and extraction a bit faster. If you need to perform additional logic when hydrating (setting) or extractling (getting) a value, however, the ClassMethods hydrator is preferred.

Zend\Stdlib\Hydrator\Reflection

This hydrator is similar to the ObjectProperty hydrator but it allows setting and getting object properties that are declared private or protected in addition to public.

Entities

Entities are classes that represent a table. The entity allows us to establish a mapping between an object and a table in the database. The user entity could look like this:

```php
<?php
namespace User\Model\Entity;

class User
{
        protected $id;
        protected $role;
        protected $name;
        protected $email;
        protected $phone;
        protected $photo;
```

---

28 http://framework.zend.com/manual/2.1/en/modules/zend.stdlib.hydrator.html

```php
/**
 * @return the $id
 */
public function getId()
{
        return $this->id;
}

/**
 * @return the $role
 */
public function getRole()
{
        return $this->role;
}

/**
 * @return the $email
 */
public function getEmail()
{
        return $this->email;
}

/**
 * @return the $phone
 */
public function getPhone()
{
        return $this->phone;
}

/**
 * @param field_type $id
 */
public function setId($id)
{
        $this->id = $id;
}

/**
 * @param field_type $role
 */
public function setRole($role)
{
        $this->role = $role;
```

```php
        }

        /**
         * @param field_type $email
         */
        public function setEmail($email)
        {
                $this->email = $email;
        }

        /**
         * @param field_type $phone
         */
        public function setPhone($phone)
        {
                $this->phone = $phone;
        }

        /**
         * @return the $name
         */
        public function getName()
        {
                return $this->name;
        }

        /**
         * @param field_type $name
         */
        public function setName($name)
        {
                $this->name = $name;
        }

        public function getPhoto()
        {
                return $this->photo;
        }

        public function setPhoto($photo)
        {
                $this->photo = $photo;
        }

}
```

In the entity we can encapsulate special logic for a property directly in the set and get methods that deal with it. Below is an example for the password property.

```
/**
 * Gets the current password hash
 *
 * @return the $password
 */
public function getPassword()
{
        return $this->password;
}

/**
 * Sets the password
 *
 * @param string $password
 */
public function setPassword($password)
{
        $this->password = $this->hashPassword($password);
}

/**
 * Verifies if the passwords match
 *
 * @param string $password
 * @return boolean
 */
public function verifyPassword($password)
{
        return ($this->password == $this->hashPassword($password));
}

/**
 * Hashes a password
 * @param string $password
 * @return string
 */
private function hashPassword($password)
{
    return md5($password);
}
```

User Entity Service

At the moment our User entity has only a base minimum of properties. What shall we do if we want to add more properties or remove existing ones? The answer encompasses at least two possible solutions. If we decide to extend this class in the future, we can either modify the user entity, or add a new module extending the properties of User. I will focus on the second solution as it improves the reusability and extensibility of the User module. We can use this module in other applications even where there is a different set of properties for users.

For this solution we only need to create a user *entity* service. The definition of this service should be added to the User module configuration as follows:

```
'service_manager' => array(
    // ...
    'invokables' => array (
        'user-entity' => 'User\Model\Entity\User',
        // ...
    )
),
```

Additionally we have to specify not to share instances for this service.

If you recall from an earlier discussion, this can be achieved by adding the shared key to the service_manager configuration:

```
'service_manager' => array(
    // ...
    'invokables' => array (
        'user-entity' => 'User\Model\Entity\User',
        // ...
    ),
    'shared' => array(
        'user-entity' => false,
    )
),
```

If you want to get the source code run these commands:

```
cd <full/path/to/>/learnzf2/
git stash
git checkout 'ch-reusability-entity'
```

Doctrine 2

Doctrine 2 is a PHP library that we will use in our application to improve its reusability. As there is a lot of information to deliver on this topic, I decided to dedicate a separate chapter to it.

When we were creating the user form, user model, and special column cases, I mentioned that any change to the database tabl e structure would have to be replicated across multiple PHP files. These files would include the table gateway class if it includes custom logic, the form definition class, and the input filter definition.

This process is extremely error prone. Lacking a solid high-level understanding of the code, it is easy to forget to add the change in all needed parts of the application. This is quite often the case when a new developer in the team starts to contribute to the project.

There are a number of solutions that overcome this problem by putting all logic pertaining to a database table class in only one file. The solution that I will cover in this chapter is based on Doctrine 2[29]. Doctrine 2 is a PHP library that provides form annotations and Object Relational Mapping (ORM) that we will use in our User module. This chapter is not an extensive Doctrine 2 tutorial: think of it more as a crash course in using the most common features of Doctrine 2 with ZF2.

Getting Started

In the composer.json file in our application we will add the following dependencies.

```
// ...
"require": {
    "php": ">=5.3.3",
    "zendframework/zendframework": "2.*",
    "doctrine/common": ">=2.1",
    "doctrine/orm": ">=2.1"
  }
}
```

After that we need to get the dependant packages using composer.

As you recall, this is done using the following commands:

```
cd /<main-application-directory>/
php composer.phar update
```

You should now have all dependant Doctrine 2 classes.

Annotating our Entity

We will add annotations to our User entity that will be used to generate form elements. Edit the module/User/src/User/Model/Entity/User.php file and make the following changes at the top:

```
<?php
namespace User\Model\Entity;
```

---

29 http://doctrine-project.org

```
use Zend\Form\Annotation;

/**
 * @Annotation\Name("users")
 * @Annotation\Hydrator("Zend\Stdlib\Hydrator\ClassMethods")
 */
class User
{
//...
```

The highlighted lines specify that we will use form annotations and the class will map to a form with name users (@Annotation\Name("users")) and to set or get the properties of the entity will use the user entity's getters and setters (@Annotation\Hydrator("Zend\Stdlib\Hydrator\Class-Methods")).

The entity contains properties that must not be shown in the form. These properties, such as the id property for example, can be excluded using the following annotation:

```
class User
{
    /**
     * @Annotation\Exclude()
     */
    protected $id;
```

Pitfalls
At the time of this writing there was one very annoying problem with annotations: using Windows line endings causes them to not work correctly. Therefore you have to convert the file to use Unix line endings. Under Linux you can fix your files using the dos2unix command line program.

Using annotations we can describe, for each form element, its HTML attributes, options, validators and filters. Below is a complete example for the phone property.

```
// ...
    /**
     * @Annotation\Type("Zend\Form\Element\Text")
     * @Annotation\Options({"label":"Your phone number:"})
     * @Annotation\Filter({"name":"StripTags"})
     * @Annotation\Filter({"name":"StringTrim"})
     * @Annotation\Validator(
     *     {"name":"RegEx", "options": {"pattern": "/^[\d-\/]+$/"}})
     * @Annotation\Attributes(
     *     {"type":"tel","required": true,"pattern": "^[\d-/]+$"})
     *
     */
    protected $phone;
// ...
```

Creating Forms from Annotations

Once we have created annotations for all properties in the entity, we can create a form based on these annotations. For that purpose we will make the following changes to our Account controller and **add** action:

```php
<?php
namespace User\Controller;

use Zend\Mvc\Controller\AbstractActionController;
use Zend\EventManager\EventManager;
use Zend\Form\Annotation\AnnotationBuilder;

class AccountController extends AbstractActionController
{
    //...

    public function addAction()
    {
        $builder = new AnnotationBuilder();
        $entity = $this->serviceLocator->get('user-entity');
        $form = $builder->createForm($entity);
        //...
```

Note that the form that is generated lacks the repeat password form element, submit button, and CSRF check. These we will have to add manually:

```php
$form->add(array(
            'name' => 'password_verify',
            'type' => 'Zend\Form\Element\Password',
            'attributes' => array(
                            'placeholder' => 'Verify Password Here...',
                            'required' => 'required',
            ),
            'options' => array(
                            'label' => 'Verify Password',
            )
    ),
);

// This is the special code that protects our form being submitted from automated scripts
$form->add(array(
            'name' => 'csrf',
            'type' => 'Zend\Form\Element\Csrf',
));

// This is the submit button
$form->add(array(
```

```
                     'name' => 'submit',
                     'type' => 'Zend\Form\Element\Submit',
                     'attributes' => array(
                                          'value' => 'Submit',
                                          'required' => 'false',
                     ),
  ));
```

There is a slight visual problem with the form. The password verify element won't be generated right after the password element, which might be confusing. At the moment in ZF2 there is no "addAfter" or "addBefore" method related to form elements, however we can use a solution which is discussed next.

First we put annotation flags before every property describing its element order. It is recommended that we use numbers incrementing in steps of one hundred.

```
/**
 ....
 * @Annotation\Flags({"priority": "500"})
 *
 * @Column(type="string")
 */
protected $email;

/**
 ...
 * @Annotation\Options({"label":"Password:", "priority": "400"})
 * @Annotation\Flags({"priority": "400"})
 *
 * @Column(type="string")
 */
protected $password;
```

For the password element specifically we will also set an option with the same number. By using steps of 100 we can easily add up to 99 elements between any two existing elements without the need to renumber the entire form. In the annotations above I used the annotations Flags and Options both with a priority of 400. The reason for using two options with the same value is that the first one, Flags, dictates the element's order in the form, but is unable to read the value from the form element. The Options annotation, on the other hand, does not have any influence on the order of the element, but the value of this annotation can be read easily from the form element later on.

The second step is to change the **add** action and specify that the **password_verify** element should have the same priority as the **password** element

```
public function addAction()
{
    $builder = new AnnotationBuilder();
    $entity = $this->serviceLocator->get('user-entity');
    $form = $builder->createForm($entity);
```

```
$form->add(array(
            'name' => 'password_verify',
            'type' => 'Zend\Form\Element\Password',
            'attributes' => array(
                            'placeholder' => 'Verify Password Here...',
                            'required' => 'required',
            ),
            'options' => array(
                            'label' => 'Verify Password',
            )
    ),
    array (
      'priority' => $form->get('password')->getOption('priority'),
      )
);
// ...
```

Binding the Form to the Entity

When you bind an object to the form, depending on the hydrator specified, the data will be read from the user entity object and used in the form to display the values. Then upon successful validation the validated values from the form will be written back to the user entity object. In our case we will use the ClassMethods hydrator, which means that reading will involve the user entity's getter methods, and writing will involve its setter methods. To bind our form to the user entity we also need to add the following code to our action method:

```
// This is the submit button
$form->add(array(
            'name' => 'submit',
            'type' => 'Zend\Form\Element\Submit',
            'attributes' => array(
                            'value' => 'Submit',
                            'required' => 'false',
            ),
));
```

```
$form->bind($entity);
```

```
if($this->getRequest()->isPost()) {
```

Once the form is submitted and the incoming data is valid the entity will contain the filtered and validated data.

Persisting an Entity

Describing Table and Column Properties

In Doctrine 2, the term persisting means saving data to a specified backend. When using Doctrine 2 you will need to indicate how to save the data. The configuration you will need to provide should include which table name and column, and how to treat the values. As with forms, this is done using annotations. In this case, however, the annotations will describe database properties. For our entity class we will specify the database table **"users"** as follows:

```
/**
 * @Annotation\Name("users")
 * @Annotation\Hydrator("Zend\Stdlib\Hydrator\ClassMethods")
 *
 * @Entity @Table(name="users")
 */
class User
{
```

For every property that needs to be persisted as a column in the database we should also specify its data type and database column attributes. For example, the id column has type integer and has to be auto-generated:

```
class User
{
    /**
     * @Annotation\Exclude()
     *
     * @Id @GeneratedValue @Column(type="integer")
     */
    protected $id;
```

The email column, on the other hand, is of type *string*:

```
    /**
     * @Annotation\Type("Zend\Form\Element\Email")
     * @Annotation\Validator({"name":"EmailAddress"})
     * @Annotation\Options({"label":"Email:"})
     * @Annotation\Attributes(
     *     {"type":"email","required": true,"placeholder": "Email Address..."})
     *
     * @Column(type="string")
     */
    protected $email;
```

If you miss annotating a property using @Column, this property will be ignored by Doctrine 2. It is extremely important to annotate all properties that need to be persisted.

Using the Entity Manager

The system that manages entities in Doctrine 2 is called the entity manager. In order to save the data we need to add the following lines:

```
$form->bind($entity);

if($this->getRequest()->isPost()) {
  $data = array_merge_recursive(
    $this->getRequest()->getPost()->toArray(),
    // make certain to merge the Files also to the post data
    $this->getRequest()->getFiles()->toArray()
  );
  $form->setData($data);
  if($form->isValid()) {
    $entityManager = $this->serviceLocator->get('entity-manager');
    $entityManager->persist($entity);
    $entityManager->flush();
```

The highlighted lines are the ones responsible for saving the data. The first highlighted line gets the Doctrine 2 entity manager. The second line "persists" (i.e. saves) the data. Doctrine 2 uses scheduling and optimization, thus the actual call to the database can be queued and executed later. If we want to save the data now, which is exactly the case here, we have to call flush.

After executing these three highlighted lines the entity will, hopefully, be successfully saved. You can later pass the entity to event triggers using the following code:

```
$event = new EventManager('user');
  $event->trigger('register', $this, array(
            'user'=> $entity,
  ));
```

Entity Manager Service

We need an *EntityManager* service that creates an instance of the Doctrine 2 entity manager. Setup configuration needs to be generated and then passed as a parameter in order to construct an entity manager, as shown in the example below:

```
use Doctrine\ORM\Tools\Setup;
use Doctrine\ORM\EntityManager as DoctrineEntityManager;

$doctrineConfig = Setup::createAnnotationMetadataConfiguration(
                              $config['doctrine']['entity_path'], true);
$entityManager = DoctrineEntityManager::create($doctrineDbConfig, $doctrineConfig);
```

The important parameters are highlighted. The first one specifies an array of paths where entity files can be found. The second parameter specifies database parameters in the form of an associative array similar to the one that is used in Zend\Db but with slight differences. Using this information we can create our entity manager service with the following code.

```php
<?php
namespace User\Service\Factory;

use Zend\ServiceManager\FactoryInterface;
use Zend\ServiceManager\ServiceLocatorInterface;

use Doctrine\ORM\Tools\Setup;
use Doctrine\ORM\EntityManager as DoctrineEntityManager;

class EntityManager implements FactoryInterface
{
    public function createService (ServiceLocatorInterface $serviceLocator)
    {
        $config = $serviceLocator->get('config');
        // The parameters in Doctrine 2 and ZF2 are slightly different.
        // Below is an example how we can reuse the db settings
        $doctrineDbConfig = (array)$config['db'];
        $doctrineDbConfig['driver'] = strtolower($doctrineDbConfig['driver']);
        if(!isset($doctrineDbConfig['dbname'])) {
            $doctrineDbConfig['dbname'] = $doctrineDbConfig['database'];
        }
        if (!isset($doctrineDbConfig['host'])) {
            $doctrineDbConfig['host'] = $doctrineDbConfig['hostname'];
        }
        if (!isset($doctrineDbConfig['user'])) {
            $doctrineDbConfig['user'] = $doctrineDbConfig['username'];
        }
        $doctrineConfig = Setup::createAnnotationMetadataConfiguration(
                                            $config['doctrine']['entity_path'], true);
        $entityManager = DoctrineEntityManager::create($doctrineDbConfig, $doctrineConfig);

        return $entityManager;
    }
}
```

Do not forget to add the service declaration in the module config file:

```php
'service_manager' => array(
    'factories' => array (
        'database'   => 'User\Service\Factory\Database',
        //...
        'entity-manager'  => 'User\Service\Factory\EntityManager',

    ),
```

In the same configuration file we will add the following configuration defining the *entity_path*:

```
'doctrine' => array(
    'entity_path' => array (
        __DIR__ . '/../src/User/Model/Entity/',
    ),
)
```

Every ZF2 module using entities and Doctrine 2 must have a similar entry in its module configuration file.

Deleting an Entity

In order to delete an entity we need to set its id and call the remove method from the entity manager. The delete action from the Account controller does exactly this:

```php
public function deleteAction()
{
    $id = $this->params ('id');
    if($id) {
        $entityManager = $this->serviceLocator->get('entity-manager');
        $userEntity = $this->serviceLocator->get('user-entity');
        $userEntity->setId($id);
        $entityManager->remove($userEntity);
        $entityManager->flush();
    }

    return array();
}
```

Finding an Entity

In our User module I will add a UserManager class that will use the entity manager to create new user entities for us based on the email address:

```php
<?php
namespace User\Model;

// ...


class UserManager implements ServiceLocatorAwareInterface
{
    // ...

    /**
     * Creates and fills the user entity identified by user identity
     * @param string $identity
     * @return Entity\User
```

```
*/
public function create($identity)
{
    $user = $this->services->get('user-entity');
    $entityManager = $this->services->get('entity-manager');

    $user = $entityManager->getRepository(get_class($user))
            ->findOneByEmail($identity);


    return $user;
}
```

The *create* method is responsible for creating a user entity. The entity's properties will be populated from the first matching database table row where the *email* column is equal to $identity. If we have another module enabled that overrides the user entity class this code will still continue to function as intended.

If we wanted to find a user with id 10, for example, we have to change the code above to something like this:

```
$user = $entityManager->getRepository(get_class($user))->findOneById($id);

// or

$user = $entityManager->getRepository(get_class($user))->find($id);
```

And if we wanted all the users having a role "admin" we can write the following code:

```
$users        =        $entityManager->getRepository(get_class($user))->findByRole('admin');
```

Direct Queries

Performance Notice

Using an ORM system to iterate over a large set of results may decrease the performance of your application. It may consume more memory than expected because an ORM system needs to create new object for every row in the result set.

In such cases it is much better to make direct SQL queries to process data.

Let's elaborate this with the following example:

Task: Get the number of all admin users that have an email address at "zend.com".

We can solve it using the following code:

```
$users = $entityManager->getRepository(get_class($user))->findByRole('admin');
$count = 0;
foreach($users as $user) {
    if(strpos($user->getEmail(),'@zend.com')!==false) {
```

```
        $count++;
    }
}
```

Although this code would probably work in our development environment, in a production environment, with thousands of users, this code would lead to severe performance problems.

For such situations Doctrine 2 has the option to create a DQL query, which is similar to an SQL query. In the DQL syntax, instead of table names we use our entity class names. The detailed explanation of DQL can be found in the Doctrine 2 manual[30]. The code above can be refactored to something like the following:

```
$query = $entityManager->createQuery("SELECT COUNT(u.id) FROM " . get_class($user) . " u
WHERE u.role = 'admin' AND u.email LIKE '%@zend.com' ");
$count = $query->getSingleScalarResult();
```

Doctrine Event Manager

When Doctrine creates entity instances it does not inject their dependencies. In order to achieve this we can implement something similar to a ZF2 service manager initializer. Let's see how this can be implemented. First, in the module configuration file, I will add the list of initializers that will be called after the initialization of an entity to the doctrine section. The User module configuration would be changed as follows:

```
'doctrine' => array(
    'entity_path' => array (
        __DIR__ . '/../src/User/Model/Entity/',
    ),
    'initializers' => array (
        // add here the list of initializers for Doctrine 2 entities
    ),
),
```

Next, to address this challenge, we can use the Doctrine event manager. We will listen to the postLoad event [31], which is triggered once the entity is initialized, and inject our dependancies at that point. At the time of this writing, the Doctrine 2 event manager is not as flexible as that of ZF2. In order to listen to the event we have to create a class with a postLoad method. We will add this class to the entity management service factory. The entity manager code will have these changes:

```
<?php
namespace User\Service\Factory;

//...
use Doctrine\Common\EventArgs;
//..
```

---

30 http://docs.doctrine-project.org/en/2.0.x/reference/dql-doctrine-query-language.html
31 http://docs.doctrine-project.org/projects/doctrine-orm/en/latest/reference/events.html

```php
use Doctrine\Common\EventArgs;

class EntityManager implements FactoryInterface
{
    public function createService (ServiceLocatorInterface $serviceLocator)
    {
        // ..
        if(isset($config['doctrine']['initializers'])) {
            $eventManager = $entityManager->getEventManager();

            foreach ($config['doctrine']['initializers'] as $initializer) {
                $eventClass = new DoctrineEvent(new $initializer(), $serviceLocator);
                $eventManager->addEventListener(\Doctrine\ORM\Events::postLoad, $eventClass);
            }
        }

        return $entityManager;
    }
}

// Quick and Dirty class to handle Doctrine 2 events
class DoctrineEvent
{
    protected $initializer;

    public function __construct($initializer, $serviceLocator)
    {
        $this->initializer = $initializer;
        $this->serviceLocator = $serviceLocator;
    }
    public function postLoad(EventArgs $event)
    {
        $entity = $event->getEntity();
        $this->initializer->initialize($entity, $this->serviceLocator);
    }
}
```

And that is how we can solve the injection problem.

Profiler

Some may complain that using an ORM may slow down code execution, and that you do not know what SQL requests are being executed. This is true if you use the ORM unwisely. In our Debug module we already measure the time needed to finish a request. To avoid execution bottlenecks, we can show SQL queries using Zend\Db components. It will be perfect if we can use the information from Doctrine 2 in the ZF2 profiler. For that purpose we need an invokable service such as module/User/src/User/Service/Invokable/DoctrineProfiler.php, shown here:

```php
<?php
namespace User\Service\Invokable;

use Zend\Db\Adapter\ParameterContainer;
use Zend\Db\Adapter\Profiler\ProfilerAwareInterface;
use Zend\Db\Adapter\Profiler\ProfilerInterface;
use Zend\Db\Adapter\StatementContainer;


use Doctrine\DBAL\Logging\SQLLogger as DoctrineProfilerInterface;

class DoctrineProfiler implements ProfilerAwareInterface, DoctrineProfilerInterface
{
    /**
     *
     * @var ProfilerInterface
     */
    protected $profiler;

        public function setProfiler(ProfilerInterface $profiler)
        {
                $this->profiler = $profiler;
        }

        /**
         * {@inheritdoc}
         */
        public function startQuery($sql, array $params = null, array $types = null)
        {
            $target = new StatementContainer($sql, new ParameterContainer((array)$params));
            $this->profiler->profilerStart($target);
        }

        /**
         * {@inheritdoc}
         */
        public function stopQuery()
        {
            $this->profiler->profilerFinish();
        }
}
```

The implementation of ProfilerAwareInterface and the *Database Profiler* initializer will guarantee that we will have access to the ZF2 profiler. We can then pass data from Doctrine 2 to the ZF2 profiler. The service definition in the module configuration is as follows:

```php
'service_manager' => array(
    'factories' => array (
       // ..
    ),
    'invokables' => array (
       // ..
       'doctrine-profiler' => 'User\Service\Invokable\DoctrineProfiler',
    )
),
```

In the entity manager service we need to make this change:

```php
<?php
namespace User\Service\Factory;

use Zend\ServiceManager\FactoryInterface;
use Zend\ServiceManager\ServiceLocatorInterface;

use Doctrine\ORM\Tools\Setup;
use Doctrine\ORM\EntityManager as DoctrineEntityManager;

class EntityManager implements FactoryInterface
{
   public function createService (ServiceLocatorInterface $serviceLocator)
   {
      $config = $serviceLocator->get('config');
      // The parameters in Doctrine 2 and ZF2 are slightly different.
      // Below is an example how we can reuse the db settings

      //...
      // attach profiler to the entity manager
      if($serviceLocator->has('doctrine-profiler')) {
         $profiler = $serviceLocator->get('doctrine-profiler');
         $entityManager->getConfiguration()->setSQLLogger($profiler);
      }

      return $entityManager;
   }
}
```

That is everything you need to do in order to profile Doctrine 2 database calls.

If you want to get the source code, type these commands:

```
cd <full/path/to/>/learnzf2/
git stash
git checkout 'ch-doctrine'
```

Better security

Logging

In order to improve the security of our User module we will log various messages.

Log Service

We will create a log service that can be reused throughout the application. The initial code of our service looks like this:

```php
<?php
namespace User\Service\Factory;
use Zend\ServiceManager\FactoryInterface;
use Zend\ServiceManager\ServiceLocatorInterface;
use Zend\Log\Logger;
use Zend\Log\Writer\Stream as StreamWriter;

class Log implements FactoryInterface
{
    public function createService (ServiceLocatorInterface $serviceLocator)
    {
        $config = $serviceLocator->get('config');
        // To start logging we need to create an instance of Zend\Log\Logger
        $log = new Logger();
        // And we must add to the logger at least on writer
        $writer = new StreamWriter('php://stderr');
        $log->addWriter($writer);

        return $log;
    }
}
```

Every log must have at least one writer. A writer represents the actual "system" where the messages will be sent. It can be a file system, mail system, or other messaging system (iOS push notifications for example). You can find the complete list of built-in writers in the ZF2 reference guide [32].

To register the service we will add the following in the service manager configuration of the User module:

```php
'service_manager' => array(
    'factories' => array (
        // ...
        'log'       => 'User\Service\Factory\Log',
    ),
```

---

32 http://framework.zend.com/manual/2.1/en/modules/zend.log.writers.html

Logging Message

Within our application, there are events that need to raise awareness. Examples of this would include when somebody is not able to log in, or when a new user is created. We could add the following code to our Log controller's inAction method to handle such events:

```
public function inAction()
    {
        // ...
        if($result->isValid()) {
            // ...

            return $this->redirect()->toRoute('user/default', array (
                'controller' => 'account',
                'action'     => 'me',
            ));
        }
        else {
            $log = $this->serviceLocator->get('log');
            $log->warn('Error logging user ['.$username.']');

        //...
        }
    }
```

Above we used the warn method. This is a shorthand form of the following

```
$log->log(Zend\Log\Logger::WARN, 'Error logging user ['.$username.']');
```

When logging a message we are required to specify the priority of the message. The ZF2 Logger component has the following built-in priorities:

```
EMERG  = 0; // Emergency: system is unusable
ALERT  = 1; // Alert: action must be taken immediately
CRIT   = 2; // Critical: critical conditions
ERR    = 3; // Error: error conditions
WARN   = 4; // Warning: warning conditions
NOTICE = 5; // Notice: normal but significant condition
INFO   = 6; // Informational: informational messages
DEBUG  = 7; // Debug: debug messages
```

The code shown earlier works for logging this specific information. But this code is not part of the core logic for the inAction method. In addition if we want to have logging in other actions we most certainly will have to copy and paste the logging code. Also, if we want to add other non-core logic after a failed log attempt, we will end up with code that is difficult to maintain and extend.

Without going into too many details, I would like to open a bracket here and mention that a coding concept called Cross Cutting Concerns (CCC), and one of the tasks of Aspect Orient-ed Programming, deals with such issues. To implement CCC in ZF2 we can do the following:

instead of putting the log code directly in the action, we will instead trigger an event. In the **Module.php** file we will attach a log listener. The refactored code looks like this:

```php
<?php
namespace User\Controller;

use Zend\Mvc\Controller\AbstractActionController;
use Zend\EventManager\EventManager;


class LogController extends AbstractActionController
{

    //..

    public function inAction()
    {
        // ...
        if($isValid) {
            // ...
            return $this->redirect()->toRoute('user/default', array (
                'controller' => 'account',
                'action'    => 'me',
            ));
        }
        else {
            $event = new EventManager('user');
            $event->trigger('log-fail', $this, array(
                            'username'=> $username
                            ));
        //...
        }
    }
    // ...
}
```

And in the User module's Module.php file we need to add the following code:

```php
public function onBootstrap(MvcEvent $event)
{
    // ...
    $sharedEventManager = $event->getApplication()->
                            getEventManager()->getSharedManager();
    $sharedEventManager->attach('user','log-fail', function($event) use ($services) {
        $username = $event->getParam('username');

        $log = $services->get('log');
```

```
    $log->warn('Error logging user ['.$username.']');
  });
}
```

Log Filters

In a development system it makes sense to see all type of messages, but in a production system it makes sense to show only the more important messages. This avoids a situation where we might be burying an important problem with debug messages! ZF2 has log filters that help us achieve this. In our log service we will use the Priority filter, adding the highlighted code:

```php
<?php
namespace User\Service\Factory;

use Zend\ServiceManager\FactoryInterface;
use Zend\ServiceManager\ServiceLocatorInterface;
use Zend\Log\Logger;
use Zend\Log\Writer\Stream as StreamWriter;
use Zend\Log\Filter\Priority as PriorityFilter;

class Log implements FactoryInterface
{
    public function createService (ServiceLocatorInterface $serviceLocator)
    {
        $config = $serviceLocator->get('config');
        // To start logging we need to create an istance of Zend\Log\Logger
        $log = new Logger();
        // And we must add to the logger at least on writer
        $writer = new StreamWriter('php://stderr');
        $log->addWriter($writer);

        $priority = @$config['log']['priority'];
        if ($priority!==null) {
            $filter = new PriorityFilter($priority);
            $writer->addFilter($filter);
        }
        return $log;
    }
}
```

The code above expects a log configuration parameter priority to be assigned. We will create a log.local.php.dist file and save it in the module/User/config/ directory. The content of the log file can be as shown below:

```php
<?php
/**
 * ...
```

```
*/
return array(
   'log' => array (
         'priority' => \Zend\Log\Logger::WARN,
   )
);
```

Remember to copy this file as **config/autoload/log.local.php** in order to activate this configuration setting.

Creating a user is another important action that needs to be logged. The listener that will do this is similar to the one that we attached to the log-fail event:

```
public function onBootstrap(MvcEvent $event)
{
   // ...

   $sharedEventManager = $event->getApplication()->
                    getEventManager()->getSharedManager();
   // ...

   $sharedEventManager->attach('user','register', function($event) use ($services) {
      $user= $event->getParam('user');

      $log = $services->get('log');
      $log->warn('Registered user ['.$user->getName().'/'.$user->getId().']');
   });
}
```

If you want to get the source code enter these commands:

```
cd <full/path/to/>/learnzf2/
git stash
git checkout 'ch-logger'
```

Zend\Crypt

Storing a password using md5 is now considered insecure. Nowadays, with the help of a powerful CPU or GPU and appropriate software, MD5 passwords can be cracked within days or even hours. The assumption that it will take years for someone to crack your MD5 hashed password is no longer valid. ZF2 comes to the rescue with the **Zend\Crypt\Password** component that can help us store passwords more securely.

Zend\Crypt\Password

The ZF2 team advises us33 to use the *Bcrypt* algorithm as the best alternative to MD5. Below is an excerpt from information provided by Enrico Zimuel, the initial creator of Zend\Crypt.

"Bcrypt is considered secure because it's very slow, the computational time of a single hash can

---

33 http://www.zimuel.it/en/english-cryptography-made-easy-with-zend-framework/

be of some seconds. That means a brute force or a dictionary attack needs huge amount of time to be completed.

The Bcrypt algorithm is implemented by the **Zend\Crypt\Password\Bcrypt** class (using the crypt() function of PHP). Here is an example of its very simple usage:

```
use Zend\Crypt\Password\Bcrypt;

$bcrypt  = new Bcrypt();
$password = $bcrypt->create('password');
printf ("Password: %s\n", $password);
```

The output of the **create()** method of Bcrypt is a string of 60 characters, which looks like this:

```
$2a$14$yuD/3v/IdbdOZ0pfIjUyJ.a0Q4Ue0UTAoES2BIgK0Op1Z6IF9.aTS
```

If we execute the example code shown above two times in a row we will obtain different outputs. The reason for this behavior is because if we don't provide a salt value, the Bcrypt class will generate a random salt each time. If you prefer to assign a salt value you can use the **setSalt()** method (the salt must be a string of at least 16 bytes).

The **Bcrypt** algorithm also needs a special cost parameter. This parameter specifies the amount of work (cycles) to run in order to elaborate the hash value. More cycles means more computational time, and consequently more security. The cost parameter is an integer value from 4 to 31. The default value is 14, that is equivalent to 1 second of computation using an Intel Core i5 CPU at 3.3 Ghz. You can specify a different cost value using the **setCost()** method. Here is an example:

```
use Zend\Crypt\Password\Bcrypt;

$bcrypt = new Bcrypt();
$bcrypt->setSalt(15);

$start  = microtime(true);
$password = $bcrypt->create('password');
$end    = microtime(true);

printf ("Password : %s\n", $password);
printf ("Exec. time: %.2f\n", $end-$start);
```

Try to execute this code snippet on your server, and observe how many seconds are needed to generate the hash value. For security reasons, I suggest using a cost value that guarantees at least 1 second of computation.

Usage Notice

Please note that if you change the cost parameter, the resulting hash will be different. This will not affect the verification process of the algorithm and will not invalidate the password hashes you already have stored. Bcrypt reads the cost parameter from the hash value, during the password authentication process. All of the parts needed to verify the hash are placed together, separated with $'s: first the algorithm, then the cost, the salt, and finally the hash.

The salt and cost parameters can also be specified, using an array, during the constructor of **Zend\Crypt\Password\Bcrypt**, as follows:

```
use Zend\Crypt\Password\Bcrypt;

$bcrypt = new Bcrypt(array(
        'salt' => '1234567890123456',
        'cost' => 16
));
```

> **Security Notice**
> It is more secure to not provide the salt. In that case the generation of the salt will be done using the random algorithm provided by ZF2.

If we want to check whether or not a password is valid against a hash value, we can use the **verify($password, $hash)** method, where $password is the value to check and $hash is the hash value generated using Bcrypt. This method returns true if the password is valid and false otherwise.

> **Usage Notice**
> Use the verify method to check passwords but do not check if the produced hashes are equal! Different salt and cost parameters produce a different hash from the same original content.

Zend\Crypt\BlockCipher

There are cases when we want to encrypt information and later decrypt back to its original form. You can do this using either *symmetric* or *asymmetric* encryption. Symmetric means that the same key is used for encryption and decryption. Asymmetric means that one key is used for encryption and another one is used for decryption. ZF2 supports both forms of encryption. For asymmetric encryption[34] there are two implemented methods: Diffie-Hellman and RSA. For symmetric encryption there is the block cipher component that allows us to use multiple symmetric algorithms. We will create a new symmetric crypto service under the Application module. The initial definition of the service is below:

```
<?php
namespace Application\Service\Factory;

use Zend\ServiceManager\FactoryInterface;
use Zend\ServiceManager\ServiceLocatorInterface;
use Zend\Crypt\BlockCipher;

class SymmetricCipher implements FactoryInterface
```

---

34 http://framework.zend.com/manual/2.1/en/modules/zend.crypt.public-key.html

```
{
  public function createService (ServiceLocatorInterface $serviceLocator)
  {
    $config = $serviceLocator->get('config');
    $blockCipher = BlockCipher::factory(
            $config['cipher']['adapter'],
            $config['cipher']['options']);
    $blockCipher->setKey($config['cipher']['encryption_key']);

    return $blockCipher;
  }
}
```

The parameters supplied to the factory method are the following:
1. *the driver name*
   The BlockCipher component uses mcrypt behind the scenes to do the real work. In our example, this is the adapter that we will specify.
2. *an array with options*
   In this array we can specify the algorithm that we want to use and its parameters.
3. *the encryption key*

This information can be added to the **module/Application/config/crypto.local.php.dist** file and might look like this:

```php
<?php
/**
* Specify here the cipher settings for your current application environment.
* If possible choose different encryption keys for your development and production
environment.
*/
return array(
        'cipher' => array(
                'adapter' => 'mcrypt',
                'options' => array(
                                'algo' => 'aes'
                ),
                'encryption_key' => '<ENTER-HERE-VERY-LONG-ENCRYPTION-KEY>',
        ),
);
```

This file has to be adapted to your application environment and copied to **config/autoload/crypto.local.php** in order to be used. Note that this is similar to what we did with the *database.local.php.dist* file in the User module.

Do not forget to register the service in the *service_manager* section:

```php
'service_manager' => array(
    'factories' => array(
      //...
      'cipher'   => 'Application\Service\Factory\SymmetricCipher',
```

```
        ),
    ),
```

This *cipher* service will be used later in the book. In order to hide the data we need to call the "encrypt" method and to unhide it we need to call "decrypt".

User Entity

The code changes in this chapter may seem too paranoid or over-engineered. If you are fine with MD5 password hashing you can skip this chapter. The chapter is helpful also as a demonstration of how to inject dependency in an entity.

Let's now change our user entity to use Zend\Crypt\Password. We can make the following changes:

```php
use Zend\Crypt\Password\Bcrypt;

class User
{
        // ...
        /**
         * Sets the password
         *
         * @param string $password
         */
        public function setPassword($password)
        {
                $this->password = $this->hashPassword($password);
        }

        /**
         * Verifies if the passwords match
         *
         * @param string $password
         * @return boolean
         */
        public function verifyPassword($password)
        {
                $bcrypt = new Bcrypt(array(
                                'cost' => 16
                ));
                return $bcrypt->verify($password, $this->password);
        }

        /**
         * Hashes a password
         * @param string $password
         * @return string
         */
```

```php
    private function hashPassword($password)
    {
        $bcrypt = new Bcrypt(array(
                'cost' => 16
        ));
        return $bcrypt->create($password);
    }
```

This solution provides better security but isn't flexible.

The changes to be shown below may seem too much for just setting different password adapters. If you are fine with the solution above, you might want to skip the rest of this chapter and start reading the next chapter.

The *salt* and *cost* parameters shown above are hard coded, which is not considered a best practice. The fact that Bcrypt is considered secure today does not mean that it will stay like this forever. What we can do is to inject the password "crypto" object directly into the user entity. For this purpose we can create a *User\Model\PasswordAwareInterface* and make the User entity implement this interface. In addition we can add a service manager initializer that will inject the password-crypt service for us. Let's see what code changes are needed. First add the User/Model/PasswordAwareInterface:

```php
<?php
namespace User\Model;

use Zend\Crypt\Password\PasswordInterface;

interface PasswordAwareInterface
{
    /**
     * Sets the password adapter
     * @param PasswordInterface $adapter
     */
    public function setPasswordAdapter(PasswordInterface $adapter);

    /**
     * Gets the password adapter
     * @return PasswordInterface
     */
    public function getPasswordAdapter();

}
```

Next, change the User entity to implement this interface:

```php
<?php
namespace User\Model\Entity;

use User\Model\PasswordAwareInterface;
use Zend\Crypt\Password\PasswordInterface;
```

```php
class User implements PasswordAwareInterface
{
    /**
     * @var PasswordInterface
     */
    protected $adapter;

    //....

    /**
     * Verifies if the provided password matches the stored one.
     *
     * @param string $password clear text password
     * @return boolean
     */
    public function verifyPassword($password)
    {
            return $this->adapter->verify($password, $this->password);
    }


    /**
     * Hashes a password
     * @param string $password
     * @return string
     */
    private function hashPassword($password)
    {
            return $this->adapter->create($password);
    }


    /**
     * Sets the password adapter
     * @param PasswordInterface $adapter
     */
    public function setPasswordAdapter(PasswordInterface $adapter)
    {
        $this->adapter = $adapter;
    }
    /**
     * Gets the password adapter
     * @return PasswordInterface
     */
    public function getPasswordAdapter()
    {
            return $this->adapter;
    }

}
```

Now create the password initializer:

```php
<?php
namespace User\Service\Factory;

use Zend\ServiceManager\FactoryInterface;
use Zend\ServiceManager\ServiceLocatorInterface;
use Zend\Crypt\Password\Bcrypt;

class PasswordAdapter implements FactoryInterface
{
    public function createService (ServiceLocatorInterface $serviceLocator)
    {
        $config = $serviceLocator->get('config');
        // Notice: In order for the code below to work make sure that you have
        // copied the module/Application/config/crypto.local.php.dist file to
        // config/autoload/crypto.local.php .
        $adapter = new Bcrypt($config['bcrypt']);

        return $adapter;
    }
}
```

Then register the initializer and the service in the module configuration file, under the *service_manager* key.

```php
'service_manager' => array(
    'factories' => array (
        //...
        'password-adapter' => 'User\Service\Factory\PasswordAdapter',

    ),
    // ...
    'initializers' => array (
        'User\Service\Initializer\Password'
    ),
),
```

And finally, we add the initialize functionality to the Doctrine initializers configuration.

```php
'doctrine' => array(
                'entity_path' => array (
                                __DIR__ . '/../src/User/Model/Entity/',
                ),
                'initializers' => array (
                            // add here the list of initializers for Doctrine 2 entities..
```

```
                       'User\Service\Initializer\Password'
        ),
    ),
```

These changes to our user entity will guarantee that we can always use the most appropriate password adapter for the current application, meeting a high standard of security compliance requirements. Now go to http://localhost/user/account/add and try to add new user. In the next chapter we will see how we can perform log in and log out for this user.

If you want to get the source code, run these commands:

```
cd <full/path/to/>/learnzf2/
git stash
git checkout 'ch-crypto'
```

Protecting our Pages

There are a number of ways we can protect the access to the web pages generated from our application. ZF2 contains some of the best components to achieve this.

Authentication

We can start implementing our page protection mechanism step by step. Usually the identity of the user is checked only once. After successful validation the identity is stored and persisted between the requests. The actual verification is done from a component called Zend\Authentication\Adapter that receives the user credentials. In most cases credentials are username and password, but can also be something else such as an International Mobile Equipment Identity (IMEI) key that is unique for each mobile phone. For subsequent requests, the stored identity is used as part of a check to see if the user has access to a given controller and action.

The initial identity check in our application will be done using the "in" action of the "Log" controller. First we will obtain an instance of the authentication service. Next we will get the authentication adapter and pass it credentials. Then we will try to authenticate the credentials.

If the authentication attempt proves valid, we will store identity information pertaining to the authenticated user. This will preclude having to ask him his username and password over and over again. The code below demonstrates these steps. The comments provide hints as to which services and methods are used to achieve this result.

In the inAction method we will read the specified username and password from the user and validate him/her. The code for inAction could look like this:

```
public function inAction()
{
    if (!$this->getRequest()->isPost())
    {
        // just show the login form
        return array();
    }

    $params = $this->getRequest()->getPost();
    $username = $params->get('username');
    $password = $params->get('password');
```

```php
$auth = $this->serviceLocator->get('auth');
$authAdapter = $auth->getAdapter();
// below we pass the username and the password to the
// authentication adapter for verification
$authAdapter->setIdentity($username);
$authAdapter->setCredential($password);

// here we do the actual verification
$result = $auth->authenticate();
$isValid = $result->isValid();
If($isValid) {
    $identity = $result->getIdentity();
    // @todo: upon successful validation store additional
    // information about him in the auth storage
}
else {
  return array('errors' => $result->getMessages());
}
}
```

If we want to log out the current user, we have to delete his identity from persistent storage. For that purpose, we can use the *clearIdentity* method from the authentication service. Here is how we can do that in the "out" action of the "Log" controller:

```php
<?php
namespace User\Controller;

use Zend\Mvc\Controller\AbstractActionController;

class LogController extends AbstractActionController
{

    public function outAction()
    {
        $auth = $this->serviceLocator->get('auth');
        $auth->clearIdentity();
        //...
    }
    // ...
}
```

Once we have our login (*inAction*) and logout (*outAction*) action methods in place, for every consecutive request we can retrieve the user's identity, and check what rights are given. The most appropriate place to tap into the application workflow would be to add listener that is executed after the route event. In the **Module.php** file we can add the following code:

```
public function onBootstrap(MvcEvent $event)
{
    // ...
    $eventManager->attach(MvcEvent::EVENT_ROUTE,
            array($this, 'protectPage'), -100);
}


public function protectPage(MvcEvent $event)
{
    $match = $event->getRouteMatch();
    if(!$match) {
        // we cannot do anything without a resolved route
        return;
    }

    $controller = $match->getParam('controller');
    $action     = $match->getParam('action');
    $namespace  = $match->getParam('__NAMESPACE__');

    // @todo:  Add here the authentication code.
}
```

In our *protectPage* method we want to allow only logged-in users access to certain pages. We can query our authentication service whether or not this user has already been identified, and if not, forward him/her to the login page. The following code additions in the *protectPage* method demonstrate how this can be achieved in ZF2:

```
public function protectPage(MvcEvent $event)
{
    $match = $event->getRouteMatch();
    if(!$match) {
        // we cannot do anything without a resolved route
        return;
    }

    $controller = $match->getParam('controller');
    $action     = $match->getParam('action');
    $namespace  = $match->getParam('__NAMESPACE__');

    $services = $event->getApplication()->getServiceManager();

    $auth = $services->get('auth');
    if (!$auth->hasIdentity()) {
        // Set the response code to HTTP 401: Auth Required
        $response = $event->getResponse();
        $response->setStatusCode(401);
```

```
    $match->setParam('controller', 'User\Controller\Log');
    $match->setParam('action', 'in');
  }
}
```

What you need to remember is that this code will be executed for all controllers in all modules. If you want to limit it only to the current module you can add a check right after getting the route match. The check can look like this:

```
// ...
  $namespace = $match->getParam('__NAMESPACE__');

  if (strpos($namespace,__NAMESPACE__)!==0) {
        return;
  }
// ...
```

Let's now create the actual authentication and authentication adapter services. ZF2 comes with component responsible for authentication called Zend\Authentication[35]. It allows us to check the identity and password of the current user, and to persist information about the identified user across requests. We will create our first authentication service and save it as **module/User/src/User/Service/Factory/Authentication.php**.

It will contain the following code:

```php
<?php
namespace User\Service\Factory;

use Zend\Authentication\AuthenticationService;
use Zend\ServiceManager\FactoryInterface;
use Zend\ServiceManager\ServiceLocatorInterface;

class Authentication implements FactoryInterface
{

    public function createService (ServiceLocatorInterface $serviceLocator)
    {
        $adapter = $serviceLocator->get('auth-adapter');

        $auth = new AuthenticationService();
        $auth->setAdapter($adapter);

        return $auth;
    }
}
```

For the authentication to work properly, we need to check user credentials against some exist-

35 http://framework.zend.com/manual/2.0/en/index.html#zend-authentication

ing system. The authentication adapter is what represents the connection to that system. ZF2 has a number of built-in authentication adapters.

If we still were using MD5 for password hashing then we could use the database adapter[36]. For the database adapter you will need to provide the following parameters:

- An instance of Zend\Db\Adapter\Adapter
- The name of the table where the username and the password are stored
- The name of the table column responsible for the username
- The name of the table field responsible for the password

Our authentication db adapter, saved as src/User/Service/Factory/AuthenticationDbAdapter.php might look like this:

```php
<?php
namespace User\Service\Factory;

use Zend\Authentication\Adapter\DbTable as DbAdapter;
use Zend\ServiceManager\FactoryInterface;
use Zend\ServiceManager\ServiceLocatorInterface;

class AuthenticationDbAdapter implements FactoryInterface
{

    public function createService (ServiceLocatorInterface $serviceLocator)
    {
        $db = $serviceLocator->get('database');
        // the 5th parameter to the constructor is
        // responsible for password treatment
        $adapter = new DbAdapter($db,
                    'users',
                    'login',
                    'password',
                    'MD5(password)');
        return $adapter;
    }
}
```

In order to be able to start using these services in our application we will have to declare them in the *service_manager* section of our **module.config.php** file. Add the following lines to it:

```php
'service_manager' = array(
    'factories' => array (
        // ...
        'auth'          => 'User\Service\Factory\Authentication',
        'auth-adapter'  => 'User\Service\Factory\AuthenticationDbAdapter',
    ),
)
```

36 http://framework.zend.com/manual/2.0/en/modules/zend.authentication.adapter.dbtable.html

You may ask yourself why we added the authentication adapter as a service and did not just hard-code it into our authentication service code. One big advantage to this approach is that we can easily switch between authentication adapters. If, in the future, for example, we wanted to authenticate against our company LDAP server, the only thing that we would need to change is the 'auth-adapter' service.

Furthermore, any changes in authentication should not be in the current module. We could create an Ldap module that overwrites the auth-adapter service. If we want to create a custom authentication adapter, the only change would be to point the 'auth-adapter' key to the new custom authentication adapter.

Creating a Custom Adapter

Let me remind you that we wanted to use a password algorithm stronger than MD5 to protect our passwords. We cannot achieve this easily with the existing DbAdapter. We can either extend the existing authentication DbAdapter, or use our own that would provide a better fit to our current application code.

I will now demonstrate for you the second option: how to create your own custom adapter. An authentication adapter needs to implement Zend\Authentiction\Adapter\AdapterInterface. Its authenticate method needs to return a result that is an instance of Zend\Authentication\Result. Because we want to get the password service from the service locator, our custom adapter also needs to implement ServiceLocatorAwareInterface. Also, in the interests of avoiding excessive code duplication, I decided to again use Doctrine 2 and the user entity methods. The final version of the custom authentication adapter could look like this.

```php
<?php
namespace User\Authentication;

use Zend\Authentication\Adapter\AbstractAdapter;
use Zend\Authentication\Result;
use Zend\ServiceManager\ServiceLocatorAwareInterface;
use Zend\ServiceManager\ServiceLocatorInterface;

class Adapter extends AbstractAdapter implements ServiceLocatorAwareInterface
{
    /**
     *
     * @var ServiceLocatorInterface
     */
    protected $serviceLocator;

        /* (non-PHPdoc)
         * @see \Zend\Authentication\Adapter\AdapterInterface::authenticate()
         */
        public function authenticate()
        {
                $entityManager = $this->serviceLocator->get('entity-manager');
                $userEntityClassName = get_class(
                        $this->serviceLocator->get('user-entity'));
                // We ask the Doctrine 2 entity manager to find a user
                // with the specified email
```

```
        $user = $entityManager->getRepository($userEntityClassName)
        ->findOneByEmail($this->identity);

        // And if we have such an user we check if his password is matching
        if ($user && $user->verifyPassword($this->credential)) {
                // upon successful validation we can
                // return the user entity object
                return new Result(Result::SUCCESS, $user);
        }

        return new Result(Result::FAILURE, $this->identity);

    }
    /* (non-PHPdoc)
     * @see \Zend\ServiceManager\ServiceLocatorAwareInterface::
     * setServiceLocator()
     */
    public function setServiceLocator(ServiceLocatorInterface $serviceLocator)
    {
            $this->serviceLocator = $serviceLocator;

    }

    /* (non-PHPdoc)
     * @see \Zend\ServiceManager\ServiceLocatorAwareInterface::
     * getServiceLocator()
     */
    public function getServiceLocator()
    {
            return $this->serviceLocator;
    }

}
```

Above is shown the authentication adapter class. If we want to use it as a service, we have to declare it in our module configuration. We can declare it in the invokables section of the service manager, as it implements *ServiceLocatorAwareInterface*. ZF2 already has an initializer that injects the service manager as long as this interface is implemented, which means that we do not need to create a separate factory class.

```
'service_manager' => array(
     'invokables' => array (
       // ..
       'auth-adapter' => 'User\Authentication\Adapter',
       // ..

     ),
//...
   ),
```

Be sure to remove the *auth-adapter* definition from the factories section, if you have added one. Finally, if you want to show a personal welcome message for the logged in user on his first request, you can add the following changes to inAction from the Log controller:

```
public function inAction()
    {
    //...
    if($isValid) {
        // upon successful validation the getIdentity method returns
        // the user entity for the provided credentials
        $user = $result->getIdentity();

        // @todo: upon successful validation store additional information about him in the auth
storage

        $this->flashmessenger()->addSuccessMessage(
            sprintf('Welcome %s. You are now logged in.',
                $user->getName()));
//...
}
```

This is enough to start protecting our pages. Type the following to get the source code:

```
cd <full/path/to/>/learnzf2/
git stash
git checkout 'ch-authentication'
```

Access Control Lists

For our User module we need to have more refined checks. We want to allow the guest to see only some areas of our website, and to grant wider access to the members, right? Access Control Lists (ACL) allow us to refine the permissions to a resource. There are three important ACL terms you will need to know:

Term	Example
Role	guest or member
Resource	account or exam
Permissions (also called: Privileges or Rights)	read, edit or delete

In ZF2 the component that can help us define such lists is Zend\Permissions\Acl [37]. In order to create new ACL we need to create the following object:

```
$acl = new Zend\Permission\Acl();
```

A resource in ZF2 can be added to the access list in the following way:

37 http://framework.zend.com/manual/2.0/en/modules/zend.permissions.acl.intro.html

```
$log = $acl->addResource('log');
$account = $acl->addResource('account');
```

There is an optional second parameter to the addResource method that allows you to create a resource that inherits from only one other resource.

For example, if we want to define a resource 'zf2test' that will inherit from a resource 'test', we can code the following:

```
$test = $acl->addResource('test');
$zftest = $acl->addResource('zftest',$test);
```

The role specifies the different type of actors in the system. The role in ACL is a container for a list of permissions specifying activities this actor is allowed perform. In our application we need a *guest* role for the visitors to our website that are not yet logged in. We also need a *member* role for the registered and logged in users. Finally, we need an admin role for the administrators of the the application.

In ZF2 it is possible to have either single or multiple inheritance in the role definition. The *member* role, for example, can inherit from guest. We could have also a *supermember* role that inherits from both guest and *member*. The definition might look like this:

```
// This is how we define the available roles
$guest = $acl->addRole('guest');
$member = $acl->addRole('member', $guest); // member inherits from guest
$admin = $acl->addRole('admin');
// Example of multiple inheritance for roles
$supermember = $acl->addRole('supermember', array($guest, $member));
```

In our application we will need the following privileges for the roles:
- Guest: can register an account, log in and see the home and about pages.
- Member: can view and edit his own account and can log in and log out.
- Admin: can do everything with every resource in our system.

We can describe this using the allow method. The first parameter for this method is the name of the role or its instance, the second is the name of the role or its instance, and the third is the list of privileges allowed:

```
$acl->allow($guest, $account, array('register));
$acl->allow($guest, $log, array('in));

$acl->allow($member, $account, array('edit'));
$acl->allow($member, $log, array('out'));

$acl->allow($admin);
```

If you do not provide the second and third parameters, or provide null as values, then the role will have the privilege to do eveything with every role in the ACL.

```
$acl->allow('admin'); // === $acl->allow('admin',null, null)
```

If you provide only the resource name as the second parameter, then that role is allowed all rights to the provided resource.

```
$acl->allow('editor','article')
```

If you provide null for the first parameter, but do provide the second and/or third parameter, then it means that every role is allowed the privileges provided in the third parameter to the resource provided as a second parameter.

```
$acl->allow(null,'log', 'in'); // every role can log in
```

Let's put the pieces together and describe the ACL for our application. In ZF2 we can describe the examples mentioned above using the following code saved as module/User/src/User/Service/FactoryAcl.php.

```php
<?php
namespace User\Service\Factory;

use Zend\ServiceManager\FactoryInterface;
use Zend\ServiceManager\ServiceLocatorInterface;
use Zend\Permissions\Acl\Acl as AccessControlList;

class Acl implements FactoryInterface
{
    public function createService (ServiceLocatorInterface $serviceLocator)
    {
        $acl  = new AccessControlList();
        // Below is how we declare the account resource
        $account = $acl->addResource('account');

        $log = $acl->addResource('log');

        // Below is how we declare the guest role
        $guest = $acl->addRole('guest');
        // .. and his permissions -
        $acl->allow($guest, $account, array('register'));
        $acl->allow($guest, $log, array('in'));

        // This is how we declare the member role
        // Notice that the member inherits the rights from the guest
        // meaning that he, like the guest, can also log in
        $member = $acl->addRole('member', $guest);
        // .. and in addition he can view his own account
        $acl->allow($member, $account, array('edit'));
        $acl->allow($member, $log, array('out'));


        // Here we define the admin
```

```
$admin = $acl->addRole('admin');
// who can do everything with the resources in the system
// the missing second and third parameters allow us to do this)
$acl->allow($admin);

    return $acl;
  }
}
```

Once the definition is ready we can use the isAllowed acl method to check rights. If we have a statement like this:

```
$acl->isAllowed('member,'log','in');
```

The component will check if the **member** role has an explicit definition saying that he is allowed or denied the in permission for the **log** resource. Such a definition does not exist in the code above. In that case the the decision will be based on the parents.

The parents are processed in reverse order. In our case we have only one parent role and that is **guest**. Guest is explicitly allowed the *in* permission for the *log* resource, thus the role *member* is also allowed. If no **allow** definition can be found then the role is denied any rights to the resource *log*.

Having the ACL coded in the Acl service will make it more difficult to extend or modify this list from other modules. What we can do is to move the ACL definition inside the module configuration. We may need to have the ACL enabled only for some modules in the application. For example we do not need an ACL for the Application module. Therefore we need to be able to enable the ACL rules per module.

Also if we want to make our User module and its ACL service usable with other applications, we may need to define in the configuration default role names for guest visitors and for logged-in users. This way other modules can override the values to fit their needs. We can have the following definition in the **User module.config.php** file:

```
'acl' => array(
    'role' => array (
      // role -> multiple parents
      'guest'  => null,
      'member' => array('guest'),
      'admin'  => null,
    ),
    'resource' => array (
      // resource -> single parent
      'account' => null,
      'log'    => null,
    ),
    'allow' => array (
      // array('role', 'resource', array('permission-1', 'permission-2', ...)),
      array('guest', 'log', 'in'),
      array('guest', 'account', 'register'),
      array('member', 'account', array('me')), // the member can only see his account
```

```
      array('member', 'log', 'out'), // the member can log out
      array('admin', null, null), // the admin can do anything with the accounts
   ),
   'deny' => array (
      array('guest', null, 'delete') // null as second parameter means
                         // all resources

   ),
   'defaults' => array (
        'guest_role' => 'guest',
        'member_role' => 'member',
   ),
   'resource_aliases' => array (
      'User\Controller\Account' => 'account',
   ),

   // List of modules to apply the ACL.
   // This is how we can specify if we have to protect the pages in our current module.
   'modules' => array (
      'User',
   ),
)
```

And our final Acl service should look like this:

```php
<?php
namespace User\Service\Factory;

use Zend\ServiceManager\FactoryInterface;
use Zend\ServiceManager\ServiceLocatorInterface;
use Zend\Permissions\Acl\Acl as AccessControlList;

class Acl implements FactoryInterface
{
    public function createService (ServiceLocatorInterface $serviceLocator)
    {
        $config = $serviceLocator->get('config');
        $aclConfig = $config['acl'];

        $acl = new AccessControlList();
        // add the defined resources
        foreach($aclConfig['resource'] as $resource=>$parent) {
            $acl->addResource($resource, $parent);
        }

        // add the defined roles
        foreach($aclConfig['role'] as $role=>$parents) {
```

```
            $acl->addRole($role, $parents);
        }

        // add the allow and deny definitions
        foreach (array('allow','deny') as $action) {
            foreach($aclConfig[$action] as $definition) {
                call_user_func_array(array($acl,$action), $definition);
            }
        }

        return $acl;
    }
}
```

Once we are ready with our ACL we will have to declare it in the service manager configuration and then use it in our *protectPage* listener. The declaration in the service manager will require us to edit the **module/User/config/module.config.php** file. In the service_manager section add the highlighted line shown below:

```
'service_manager' => array(
    'factories' => array (
        //...
        'auth'      => 'User\Service\Factory\Authentication',
        'acl'       => 'User\Service\Factory\Acl',
    )
)
```

Now let's improve our *protectPage* method and enable access control. First we will check if this module needs to have access control enabled for its controller actions. Then we need to get the current user's role from the authentication service. Finally, we have to get the acl service to tell us if the current user role is allowed to do something with the resource.

In this example, the controller name will be our *resource*, and the action name will be the *privilege*. This way when the current user tries to open the */user/account/register* page we can re-phrase his action with the following question: "Is the current user with role guest allowed to register an account?" The code that implements this question using ACL looks like this:

```
$acl->isAllowed('guest','account','register');
```

We can add the following code at the end of the protectPage method:

```
public function protectPage(MvcEvent $event)
{
        $match = $event->getRouteMatch();
        if(!$match) {
                // we cannot do anything without a resolved route
                return;
        }

        $controller = $match->getParam('controller');
```

```php
$action    = $match->getParam('action');
$namespace = $match->getParam('__NAMESPACE__');

$parts          = explode('\\', $namespace);
$moduleNamespace = $parts[0];

$services = $event->getApplication()->getServiceManager();
$config = $services->get('config');

// check if the current module wants to use the ACL
$aclModules = $config['acl']['modules'];
if (!empty($aclModules) && !in_array($moduleNamespace, $aclModules)) {
        return;
}


$auth    = $services->get('auth');
$acl     = $services->get('acl');

// setup default roles for the current user
$role = $config['acl']['defaults']['guest_role'];
if($auth->hasIdentity()) {
        $user = $auth->getIdentity();
        $role = $user->getRole();
        if(!$role) {
                $role = $config['acl']['defaults']['member_role'];
        }
}


// Get the short name of the controller and use it as resource name
// Example: User\Controller\Course -> course
$resourceAliases = $config['acl']['resource_aliases'];
if (isset($resourceAliases[$controller])) {
        $resource = $resourceAliases[$controller];
}
else {
        $resource = strtolower(substr($controller, strrpos($controller,'\\')+1));
}

// If a resource is not in the ACL add it
if(!$acl->hasResource($resource)) {
        $acl->addResource($resource);
}
try {
        if($acl->isAllowed($role, $resource, $action)) {
                return;
        }
}
```

```
catch(AclException $ex) {
        // @todo: log in the warning log the missing resource
}

// If the role is not allowed access to the resource we have to redirect the
// current user to the log in page.

// Set the response code to HTTP 403: Forbidden
$response = $event->getResponse();
$response->setStatusCode(403);
// and redirect the current user to the denied action
$match->setParam('controller', 'User\Controller\Account');
$match->setParam('action', 'denied');
}
```

In order for the code above to work, make sure that you have *defined* a denied action in the account controller. This method should display a polite message saying that the user is not allowed to access this page.

We will make one small improvement to the code shown above. You may have noticed that the code which specifies the default role of a user is logically more appropriate in a service called user that will represent the currently logged-in user. Add the following change to the *protect-Page* method:

```
$acl    = $services->get('acl');

// get the role of the current user
$currentUser = $services->get('user');
$role = $currentUser->getRole();

// Get the short name of the controller and use it as resource name
// Example: User\Controller\Course -> course
$resourceAliases = $config['acl']['resource_aliases'];
```

Assuming the service has been added to the service manager configuration, our *user* service will have the following code:

```php
<?php
namespace User\Service\Factory;

use Zend\ServiceManager\FactoryInterface;
use Zend\ServiceManager\ServiceLocatorInterface;

class User implements FactoryInterface
{
        public function createService(ServiceLocatorInterface $serviceLocator)
        {
            $config = $serviceLocator->get('config');
            $auth = $serviceLocator->get('auth');
```

```
        if($auth->hasIdentity()) {
                $user = $auth->getIdentity();
                if(!$user->getRole()) {
                    $user->setRole($config['acl']['defaults']['member_role']);
                }
        }
        else {
                $user = $serviceLocator->get('user_entity');
                $user->setId(null);
                $user->setRole($config['acl']['defaults']['guest_role']);
        }

        return $user;
    }
}
```

Having now created our improved version, it is time to look at testing.

Testing our Changes

We have already defined a PHPUnit test that checks the account controller. Run it to see if everything is still working properly.

```
ZF2_PATH=`pwd`/vendor/zendframework/zendframework/library \
php vendor/bin/phpunit -c module/User/tests/
```

It should fail with an error message similar to this one: *"AccountControllerTest::testMeAction Failed asserting action name "me", actual action name is "denied"* ". Do you know why? Because of our newly defined access control list, running the test as a normal guest user will not allow us to go to the Account controller and me action. Accordingly, we need to get the current user and make some adjustments:

```
    public function testMeAction()
    {
        $application = $this->getApplication();
        $serviceManager = $application->getServiceManager();
        // ...

        $user = $serviceManager->get('user');
        $user->setRole('member');

        // The dispatch method returns the result.
        $result = $this->dispatch('/user/account/me');

        $this->assertActionName('me');
        $this->assertControllerName('User\Controller\Account');
        //...
    }
```

Notice how we gain access to the service manager: through the MVC *Application* instance.

At the moment the "member" role is hard coded. We can improve the test by taking this role from the service manager config and using it in the test as follows:

```php
public function testMeAction()
{
    $application = $this->getApplication();
    $serviceManager = $application->getServiceManager();
    // ...

    $user = $serviceManager->get('user');
    $config = $serviceManager->get('config');
    $user->setRole($config['acl']['defaults']['member_role']);

    $result = $this->dispatch('/user/account/me');

    $this->assertActionName('me');
    $this->assertControllerName('User\Controller\Account');
    //...
}
```

If you were not able to follow the code changes, or they did not work for you, get the source for the chapter with the commands below:

```
cd <full/path/to/>/learnzf2/
git stash
git checkout 'ch-acl'
```

Navigation

It will be great if we can make the navigation menu of our application change automatically depending on which modules are enabled. This is possible in ZF2 and the steps you will need to follow are covered in the paragraphs below.

Defining Module Navigation

For every module that needs to have menu items, in its module configuration file, we can add a **navigation** key and describe the items. In the User module we can start describing the menu items as shown below:

```
'navigation' => array(
    'default' => array(
        array(
            'label' => 'User',
            'route' => 'user/default',
            'controller'=> 'account',
            'pages' => array(
                array(
//...
```

The "default" key in the second line above specifies the unique name of this navigation set. Under the default we have one array per menu item.

In this example the menu item "default" is represented by an array with the following *keys* and values:

- *label:* assigned a value of "User"
- *route:* assigned a parent/child route "user/default"
- *controller:* assigned to "account"

Under the "pages" key we can define sub-items for this menu, such as the following:

```
'pages' => array(
    array(
        'label' => 'Me',
        'route' => 'user/default',
        'controller' => 'account',
        'action' => 'me',
    ),
    array(
        'label' => 'Add',
        'route' => 'user/default',
        'controller' => 'account',
        'action' => 'add',
    ),
```

When defining an item it is important to define the label and the URL of the item. If we want to use the routing table to generate the URL for us, then we must at least add a "route" key.

If the route accepts parameters we should pass also the correct parameters to generate the URL. If you want to point the item directly to a specific URL you can use the "uri" parameter. For the navigation definition in the Application module we have the following code:

```
'navigation' => array(
    'default' => array(
        array(
                'label' => 'Home',
                'route' => 'home',
                'pages' => array (
                array(
                    'label' => 'About',
                    'route' => 'application/default',
                    'controller' => 'index',
                    'action' => 'about'
                ),
                 array(
                    'label' => 'Book',
                    'uri'  => 'http://learnzf2.com',
                )
            )
        ),
    )
),
```

Enabling Navigation

Once we have the initial per module definition, we need to define the navigation service. We will do this in our Application module.

Module Organization Notice

We do not place the navigation service in the User module because it is not logically connected with the User. The User module is only responsible for user management. Such responsibilities include allowing them to log in or to log out, protecting pages based on their role, etc. It would be better to configure the navigation service among services provided by the Application module.

The code should be as follows:

```
'service_manager' => array(
    'factories' => array(
        'translator' => 'Zend\I18n\Translator\TranslatorServiceFactory',
        // ...
        'navigation' => 'Zend\Navigation\Service\DefaultNavigationFactory',
    ),
),
```

Now we are ready to render the navigation menus.

Rendering Navigation

The ZF2 navigation component includes view plugins that help us display normal and bread-crumb menus, site maps, and more[38]. For our application we will display breadcrumbs for the active menu. We will also change the current hard-coded menu to be more flexible. The first changes to **layout.phtml** in the Application module are as follows:

```
<div class="navbar navbar-inverse navbar-fixed-top">
 <div class="navbar-inner">
 <!—- the hard coded menu à
 </div>
 <div class="breadcrumb">
      <!-- Breadcrumb navigation -->
     <?php
      echo $this->navigation('navigation')->breadcrumbs()->setMinDepth(1)->setSeparator('
 ' . PHP_EOL);
     ?>
 </div>
</div>
```

We can replace the hard-coded menu with the following code:

```
<?php
echo $this->navigation('navigation')
     ->menu()
     ->setMinDepth(1);
?>
```

Container and Pages

Because the skeleton application for ZF2 uses the *Twitter Bootstrap*[39] JavaScript library we would like to take full advantage of it in order to generate nicer menus. Unfortunately the de-fault menu view helper does not have the flexibility that we need, so we will have to generate the menu after retrieving menu information from the navigation container.

In ZF2, navigation items are organized in a hierarchy of **container** and **pages**. Every container may have one or more pages. The pages are the top level items. The code below demonstrates how to access the container and its pages in the view.

```
    $navHelper = $this->navigation('navigation');
    $containers = $navHelper->getContainer();
    foreach($containers->getPages() as $page) {
//...
```

For every page we can access the label (*href* attribute), check if the page is active or accepted, among other properties. Every page may have sub-pages. These can be accessed with code

---

38 http://framework.zend.com/manual/2.1/en/modules/zend.navigation.view.helpers.html
39 http://twitter.github.com/bootstrap/

such as this:

```php
$navHelper = $this->navigation('navigation');
$containers = $navHelper->getContainer();
foreach($containers->getPages() as $page) {
    //..

    if(count($page)) {
        // if there are subpages we render the menu a bit different
        $label  = $page->getLabel();
        //..
        foreach($page as $subPage) {
            if(!$navHelper->accept($subPage)) {
                continue;
            }
            // ...
```

Finally notice that the code below can be used ...

```php
<div class="nav-collapse collapse">
    <ul class="nav">
    <?php
        $navHelper = $this->navigation('navigation');
        $containers = $navHelper->getContainer();
        foreach($containers->getPages() as $page) {
            $class = "";
            if ($page->isActive()) {
                $class = "active";
            }

            if(count($page)) {
                // if there are subpages we render the menu a bit different
                $label  = $page->getLabel();
                $label  = $this->translate($label); // translated label
                $label  = $this->escapehtml($label); // sanitized label
                printf('<li class="dropdown%s">'."\n",
                    ($class?' '.$class:'')
                );
                printf(' <a href="%s" class="dropdown-toggle" data-toggle="dropdown">%s<b
class="caret"></b></a>'."\n",
                    $page->getHref(),
                    $label
                );
                echo '<ul class="dropdown-menu">'."\n";
                foreach($page as $subPage) {
                    if(!$navHelper->accept($subPage)) {
                        continue;
```

```
                }
            printf("<li>%s</li>\n",$navHelper->htmlify($subPage));
                    }
            echo "</ul></li>\n";
        }
        else {
            printf("<li class=\"%s\">%s</li>\n",
                $class,$navHelper->htmlify($page));
            }
        }
    ?>
    </ul>
</div>
```

… to display the nice navigation structure shown below:

Adding ACL

Depending on the current user's role, it may be appropriate to show or to hide different menu items. For that purpose we can use an ACL (Access Control List). For every item in the menu we can define a resource and, if needed, a privilege. The following configuration, under the *default* navigation key, defines a login page menu item. This item will be displayed only to users whose role is allowed the **in** privilege for the **log** resource.

```
'navigation' => array(
   'default' => array(
      array(
         'label' => 'User',
         'route' => 'user/default',
         'controller'=> 'account',
         'pages' => array(
            //...

            array(
                    'label' => 'Log in',
               // uri
                    'route' => 'user/default',
                    'controller' => 'log',
                    'action'   => 'in',
               // acl
               'resource'  => 'log',
               'privilege' => 'in'
            ),
```

```
        )
      )
    ),
// ..
```

In order to pass the current role and ACL to the navigation view plugins we can use the following code in the **module/User/Module.php** file:

```
public function protectPage(MvcEvent $event)
{
        $match = $event->getRouteMatch();
        if(!$match) {
                // we cannot do anything without a resolved route
                return;
        }
        //...

        $auth   = $services->get('auth');
        $acl    = $services->get('acl');

        // get the role of the current user
        $currentUser = $services->get('user');
        $role = $currentUser->getRole();

        // This is how we add default acl and role to the navigation view helpers
        \Zend\View\Helper\Navigation\AbstractHelper::setDefaultAcl($acl);
        \Zend\View\Helper\Navigation\AbstractHelper::setDefaultRole($role);
        // check if the current module wants to use the ACL
        $aclModules = $config['acl']['modules'];
        if (!empty($aclModules) && !in_array($moduleNamespace, $aclModules)) {
                return;
        }
        //...
}
```

Notice that I moved the code which checks if this module is using *acl* for protecting its pages further down. If I had not moved that block of code, the navigation would have shown all available items when a user accessed a page from a module with no ACL definition.

Security Notice:
Specifying the ACL for a menu item means only that it will be shown or hidden depending on the role of the current user. This does not prevent a user from accessing a hidden menu item by directly typing the URL from the browser. For that purpose you can also define ACL rules to allow or deny access to the pages themselves.

If you want to get the source code, type these commands:

```
cd <full/path/to/>/learnzf2/
git stash
git checkout 'ch-navigation'
```

Analyzing our Modules

So far we have created two modules, and also improved the Application module included with the ZF2 Skeleton Application. Before we proceed to the next module, it is time to stop for a moment, and to analyze our code as it stands right now. The modules must first pass the criteria for best practices defined in the beginning.

Any given module must ...
- be self-contained
- have a clear purpose
- implement logically grouped functionality
- be simple to use and extend
- allow loose coupling

Debug Module

Be Self-Contained

The check for self containment is pretty straight forward. You have to disable the Debug module and the application should continue to function, obviously without the Debug functionality. Go to the **config/autoload.application.config.php** file and comment out the line which enables the Debug module.

```php
<?php
return array(
    // This should be an array of module namespaces used in the application.
    'modules' => array(
        'Application',
        //'Debug',
        'User',
        'Exam',
    ),
//..
)
```

Now you can reload the web application in the browser and randomly access different pages to see if the application continues to function. If you followed the chapters in this book then the Debug module should pass the self-containment condition. The reason for this is that when the module is disabled, its event listeners are not executed. Of course there is no debug overlay, no database profiling information, and no error log reporting on request execution time, and so forth.

Passing the self-containment criteria for the Debug module brings a lot of advantages. For example, when we move our application to the production server, we only need to disable the Debug module, and the rest of the code will function as before, without the overhead involved in performing calculations, capturing data and writing to files.

Has a Clear Purpose

The purpose for the Debug module is quite clear: it is responsible for providing debug information on our application. It provides debug information on modules, MVC execution times,

SQL queries, database interaction, etc. In this respect, our Debug module clearly matches the second criterion.

Implements Logically Grouped Functionality

The functionality of the Debug module is represented by methods which calculate execution times, collect information about loaded modules, time the performance of SQL queries, and gather SQL parameter information. We can agree that these methods are all logically related. Even the overlay that we implemented is logically grouped with this functionality as it allows us to also display debug information in the browser. Accordingly, it is clear that the Debug module classes and methods implement logically grouped functionality.

Be Simple to Use and Extend

In order to use it we just need to have its source code available, and to enable it in the application config file. Enable this module again (if you disabled it to check for self containment): we will still need it for future development.

Although the module is easy to use, "documentation" is lacking. Some aspects of the application are configurable. For example, if there is a database profiler service, it is expected to be called *database-profiler*. If that is not the case then we can easily add an alias that points to the current name of the profiler services. In order to match this criterion we have to add a description of this expectation. You could add it in the **module.config.php** file as commented text at the top, or create a file called **module/Debug/config/debug.global.php.dist** that has the following code:

```php
<?php
return array(
// The Debug module expects the database service to be called "database".
// If that is not the case add a service alias that points to the correct name.
        'service_manager' => array(
// This line is an example how to alias it if the correct name of the service
// is Zend\Db\Adapter\Profiler\Profiler
            'alias' => array(
                'database-profiler' => 'Zend\Db\Adapter\Profiler\Profiler',
            ),
        )
);
```

I will advise you to use this latter approach. If someone wants to use our Debug module and to configure it according to the application setup, he can see in the "dist" file any expectations of the Debug module.

At the moment the debug overlay is the only view template in the Debug module. And if someone uses the Debug module and wants to provide his own debug overlay it is not very clear what is the view template name and where is the actual file. Therefore, it will be better to provide the following definition in the **debug.global.php.dist** configuration file:

```php
<?php
return array(
  'service_manager' => array(
//...
  ),
  'view_manager' => array(
```

```
'template_map' => array(
    // This is the debug template that surrounds the page.
    // You can change the value of the key to point to a view template
    // file that is more shiny.
    'debug/layout/sidebar' => __DIR__ . '/../view/debug/layout/sidebar.phtml',
)
),
```

The only functionality exported by this module exports is the *timer* service and the *database-profiler* initializer. Because these are defined in the service manager configuration, they can be easily extended or replaced with something better.

Allows Loose Coupling

As this module does not trigger any events, this criterion is not applicable.

User Module

Be Self-Contained

To test this criterion, we have to disable the User module and see if our application still works. Apart from the missing user controllers, the rest should continue to function. Assuming that the Debug module has been re-enabled, its overlay should also be visible. The navigation should have a *Home* item and the *User* item should not be visible. Finally, the ACL for the pages is disabled. It would seem that this module also passes the *self-contained* criterion without the need for any changes.

Has a Clear Purpose

The User module provides user management and protection for the pages based on the current user. Accordingly, we can confidently state that this module has a clear purpose.

Implements Logically Grouped Functionality

This module implements functionality that matches its purpose: user management, authentication and ACL. It is possible to have a dedicated ACL module that is built on top of the User module, but for our purposes this ACL is sufficient. The User module does not provide navigation as this is the responsibility of the Application module.

If there were a "Crypto" module, its responsibility would be to provide the cipher service. For simplicity I did not want to introduce another module, therefore the Application module was the next best choice to house the cipher service. On the other hand the *password-adapter* service is an integral part of User module functionality, and its presence therefore does not violate this criterion.

Be Simple to Use and Extend

The User module requires a database to be created in order to work. It would be a good idea to add this information to the **README.md** file. It will be even better if we had a way to automate module installation. When we start discussing *composer* in detail you will see how to achieve this. For the moment we will say that there is still some work to do in order to pass this criterion.

If we want to use this module in another application where the user has completely different properties then we need to create another user entity class with the correct annotations. We would also then need to add a service manager application definition that overwrites the existing user entity definition, and points to the new user entity class. We do not need to overwrite the form because it will be up to date with the user entity used. The authentication adapter need not be overwritten either, as long as the email is the identity. If that is not the case we can overwrite the auth-adapter service with one that works with our new user entity.

Finally, if we want to use another password adapter for the user, we can overwrite the *password-adapter* service. Our User module is quite flexible in that aspect. The other functionality related to page protection is also exposed via services and can be overwritten to match the application requirements. What we can improve is to add more information in the **README.md** file describing this.

Allows Loose Coupling

This module triggers events in cases where a new user is registered or when a user cannot log in. This contributes to the concept of loose coupling with other modules and allows them to hook into these events, adding extra functionality. It will be a good idea to also trigger an event when the current user is denied access to a page and describe the events that are triggered in the **README.md** file.

This section in the book has shown you a brief analysis of our modules, as well as information on how to improve them.

To get the source code for changes suggested in this chapter, run the following commands:

```
cd <full/path/to/>/learnzf2/
git stash
git checkout 'ch-module-check'
```

Exam Module

The Exam module, our final module for the book, will allow registered users to take tests in different subjects. We will dig deeper into form definition, creating custom form elements and building custom view helpers to assist with form rendering. In the area of database access, we will see how to paginate our results. Finally, we will demonstrate how to generate a PDF certificate of excellence and send it via email when a user passes an exam.

You have to create for yourself the initial version of the Exam module, or you could get it from the source code accompanying the book:

```
cd <full/path/to/>/learnzf2/
git stash
git checkout 'ch-exam-skeleton'
```

Advanced Form Usage

Custom Form Elements

In the Exam module we need to be able to generate exam forms which contain different types of questions. For simplicity we will add the most common types of questions that are present on an exam:

- multple choice
- single choice
- yes/no (also known as true/false)
- free text

We will save the form elements that represent the different question types in the folder **module/Exam/src/Form/Element/**. The question form elements are slightly different than a normal form element because they are composite elements. A single question element can consist of a container for the possible answers, a field for question text, and a question header. Furthermore, we have to be able to pass to the form the correct answers for validation. To distinguish our form elements we will create an interface **QuestionInterface.php**:

```php
<?php
namespace Exam\Form\Element\Question;

interface QuestionInterface
{
  /**
   * Specifies the question
   * @param string $text
   */
        public function setQuestion($text);

        /** Gets the question text
         * @return string
         */
        public function getQuestion();

        /**
         * Specifies the header text
         * @param string $text
         */
        public function setHeader($text);

        /** Gets the question header
         * @return string
         */
        public function getHeader();

        /**
         * Sets the answer(s)
```

```php
 * @param array|string $answers
 */
public function setAnswers($answers);
}
```

The initial version of **MultipleQuestion.php** can implement the *QuestionInterface* and extend the already existing *MultipleChoice* form element:

```php
<?php
namespace Exam\Form\Element\Question;

use Zend\Form\Element\MultiCheckbox;
use Zend\Validator\ValidatorInterface;
use Zend\Form\Exception\InvalidArgumentException;
use Zend\Validator\Callback;

class MultipleChoice extends MultiCheckbox implements QuestionInterface
{
    protected $question;
    protected $answers;
    protected $header = 'Only %d of the following answers %s correct.';
    protected $maxAnswers = null;

    /**
     * Specifies the question
     * @param string $text
     */
    public function setQuestion($text)
    {
        $this->question = $text;
    }

    /**
     * Specifies the header text
     * @param string $text
     */
    public function setHeader($text)
    {
        $this->header = $text;
    }

    /** Gets the question text
     * @return string
     */
    public function getQuestion()
    {
        return $this->question;
```

```
        }

        /** Gets the question header
         * @return string
         */
        public function getHeader()
        {
           $count = count($this->answers);
           return sprintf($this->header, $count, $count>1?'are':'is');
        }

        /**
         * Sets the answer(s)
         * @param array|string $answers
         */
        public function setAnswers($answers)
        {
           $answers = (array)$answers;
           if (empty($answers) ||
              (null !== $this->maxAnswers &&
              count($answers) > $this->maxAnswers)) {
                  throw new InvalidArgumentException('Invalid number of correct answers');
           }

           $this->answers = $answers;
        }

        /**
         * Gets the list of answers
         * @return array
         */
        public function getAnswers()
        {
                  return $this->answers;
        }
        // ...
}
```

We want to have default validators for the element that check if the provided input from the users matches all answers. For that reason we must override the *getValidator* method.

```
        /**
         * Get validator
         *
         * @return ValidatorInterface
         */
        protected function getValidator()
        {
```

```
            if (null === $this->validator) {
                $answers = $this->getAnswers();
                // Example: Custom Validator Via Callback
                $this->validator = new Callback(function($value) use ($answers) {
                        $diff = array_diff($answers, $value);
                        if(!empty($diff)) {
                                return false;
                        }
                        return true;
                });
            }
            return $this->validator;
    }
```

In the future we would like to have a form builder that can help us create new tests. For that reason we must be able to create such an element using form specification. In order to be able to pass the parameters we need to override *setOptions*:

```
    /**
    * Set options for an element. Accepted options are:
    * - label: label to associate with the element
    * - label_attributes: attributes to use when the label is rendered
    * - value_options: list of values and labels for the select options
    *
    * @param  array|\Traversable $options
    * @return MultiCheckbox|ElementInterface
    * @throws InvalidArgumentException
    */
    public function setOptions($options)
    {
            parent::setOptions($options);

            if (isset($this->options['question'])) {
                    $this->setQuestion($this->options['question']);
            }
            if (isset($this->options['header'])) {
                    $this->setHeader($this->options['header']);
            }
            if (isset($this->options['answers'])) {
                    $this->setAnswers($this->options['answers']);
            }

            return $this;
    }
```

That should be enough for adding a *multiple choice* question to an exam form. For the *single choice* question the code is the following:

```php
<?php
namespace Exam\Form\Element\Question;

class SingleChoice extends MultipleChoice
{
    protected $maxAnswers = 1;
}
```

The *yes/no* question element looks like this:

```php
<?php
namespace Exam\Form\Element\Question;

class YesNo extends SingleChoice
{
    protected $header = 'Is this correct?';

    public function init()
    {
        parent::setValueOptions(array(
            '0' => 'No',
            '1' => 'Yes',
        ));
    }

    /**
     * @param  array $options
     * @return MultiCheckbox
     */
    public function setValueOptions(array $options)
    {
        throw new \Exception('This method is not allowed');
    }

    /**
     * Set options for an element. Accepted options are:
     * - label: label to associate with the element
     * - label_attributes: attributes to use when the label is rendered
     *
     * @param  array|\Traversable $options
     * @return YesNo|ElementInterface
     * @throws InvalidArgumentException
     */
    public function setOptions($options)
    {
        parent::setOptions($options);
```

```php
        return $this;
    }
}
```

And finally the *free text* form element looks like this

```php
<?php
namespace Exam\Form\Element\Question;

class FreeText extends SingleChoice
{
    protected $header = 'Enter the answer in the text field';

    /**
     * (non-PHPdoc)
     * @see \Exam\Form\Element\Question\MultipleChoice::setAnswers()
     */
    public function setAnswers($answers)
    {
            parent::setAnswers($answers);
            foreach($this->answers as &$answer) {
                    $answer = strtolower($answer);
            }
    }

    /**
     * Provide default input rules for this element
     *
     * Attaches an email validator.
     *
     * @return array
     */
    public function getInputSpecification()
    {
        return array(
            'name' => $this->getName(),
            'required' => true,
            'filters' => array(
                array('name' => 'Zend\Filter\StringTrim'),
                array('name' => 'Zend\Filter\StringToLower'),
            ),
            'validators' => array(
                $this->getValidator(),
            ),
        );
    }
}
```

So far, so good. Now we want to describe a complete exam using these new form elements.

Form Factories

In ZF2 you can create a complete form using Zend\Form\Factory and form specification. The specification is an array with a special format which must describe the form and its elements. The array might also potentially describe field sets and input filters. We will create a sample questionnaire and save it as **module/Exam/config/form/form1.php**. The following array is a valid form specification with one question element:

```php
$i = 0;
return array(
    'type' => 'form',
    'elements' => array(
            array(
                    'spec' => array(
                            'type' => 'Exam\Form\Element\Question\SingleChoice',
                            'name' => 'q'.++$i,
                            'options' => array(
                                    'value_options' => array(
                                            'namespaces' => 'namespaces',
                                            'classes' => 'classes',
                                            'traits' => 'traits',
                                            'multi' => 'multiple inheritance'
                                    ),
                                    'question' => 'What is new in PHP 5.4',
                                    'answers' => array(
                                            'traits'
                                    )
                            )
                    )
            ),
    // ...
);
```

We can add to the array additional information that is not form specific, but will be used to describe the test itself:

```php
$i = 0;
return array(
    'info' => array(
        'name' => 'PHP 5 test',
        'locale' => 'en_US',
        'description' => 'Tests your PHP 5 knowledge',
        'creator' => 1,
        'active' => 1,
        'duration' => 30,
    ),
```

'type' => 'form',

Once we are ready with the specification we can use the Form Factory. In the *TestController* we will add a method *takeAction* that will be responsible for reading the *id* indicating the definition of the exam to be displayed. The initial version of our *takeAction* method can look like the one below:

```php
<?php
namespace Exam\Controller;
// ...
use Zend\Form\Factory;

class TestController extends AbstractActionController
{
    //...
    public function takeAction()
    {
        $id = $this->params('id');
        if(!$id) {
            return $this->redirect()->toRoute('exam/list');
        }

        $factory = new Factory();
        $spec = include __DIR__.'/../../../config/form/form1.php';
        $form = $factory->create($spec);
        return array('form' => $form);
    }
}
```

In order to display these custom form elements we also need custom view plugins.

Custom View Plugins

The custom view plugins needed will render for display the different question elements that we have devised. These view plugins will be saved in **module/Exam/src/Exam/Form/View/Helper/Question**. We need a view plugin to render our single choice, multiple choice and free text question types. A yes/no question can be rendered using the single choice plugin. We will also create a view plugin called *FormQuestionElement* that will be able to handle question elements and decide which view helper to use.

In order to create a custom view helper we have to extend from Zend\View\Helper\Abstract and we need to implement the __*invoke* and *render* methods. The initial version of our *FormQuestionElement* is shown below:

```php
<?php
namespace Exam\Form\View\Helper\Question;

use Zend\Form\View\Helper\AbstractHelper;
use Exam\Form\Element\Question\QuestionInterface;

class FormQuestionElement extends AbstractHelper
```

```
{
  /**
   * Invoke helper as functor
   *
   * Proxies to {@link render()}.
   *
   * @param  ElementInterface|null $element
   * @return string|FormInput
   */
  public function __invoke(QuestionInterface $element = null)
  {
    if (!$element) {
        return $this;
    }

    return $this->render($element);
  }

  /**
   * Render
   *
   * @param QuestionInterface $element
   * @param array             $options
   * @param array             $selectedOptions
   * @param array             $attributes
   * @return string
   */
  public function render(QuestionInterface $element)
  {
    // ...

    return $content;
  }
}
```

The *render* method must return the rendered text.

It is possible from one view plugin to access other view plugins. This is done via the view object. The final version of our render method should look like this:

```
  /**
   * Render
   *
   * @param QuestionInterface $element
   * @param array             $options
   * @param array             $selectedOptions
   * @param array             $attributes
   * @return string
```

```
    */
    public function render(QuestionInterface $element)
    {
        $view = $this->getView();
        if ($element instanceof \Exam\Form\Element\Question\FreeText) {
            $content = $this->view->formFreeText($element);
        }
        else if($element instanceof \Exam\Form\Element\Question\SingleChoice) {
            $content = $this->view->formSingleChoice($element);
        }
        else {
            $content = $this->view->formMultipleChoice($element);
        }

        return $content;
    }
```

Once we are ready with the view plugin we need to register it so that ZF2 can use it. We have to add a 'view_helpers' section to the module configuration:

```
//..
'view_helpers' => array (
    'invokables' => array (
        'formMultipleChoice'  => 'Exam\Form\View\Helper\Question\FormMultipleChoice',
        'formSingleChoice'   =>
'Exam\Form\View\Helper\Question\FormSingleChoice',
        'formFreeText'       =>
'Exam\Form\View\Helper\Question\FormFreeText',
        'formQuestionElement' =>
'Exam\Form\View\Helper\Question\FormQuestionElement',
    )
),
// ...
```

The code for the free text view plugin is relatively straight forward:

```
<?php
namespace Exam\Form\View\Helper\Question;

use Zend\Form\View\Helper\FormText;
use Exam\Form\Element\Question\FreeText;

class FormFreeText extends FormText
{
    /**
     * Render
     *
     * @param MultiCheckboxElement $element
```

```php
 * @param array            $options
 * @param array            $selectedOptions
 * @param array            $attributes
 * @return string
 */
public function render(FreeText $element)
{
  $question = $element->getQuestion();
  $header  = $element->getHeader();

  $content  = "<dd><pre>"
      . $this->getView()->escapeHtml($question)
      . "</pre></dd>";
  $content .= "<dl>$header</dl>";
  $content .= parent::render($element);

  return $content;
  }
}
```

In the code above we extend from Zend\Form\Element\FormText and therefore do not have to implement __invoke.

The multiple choice plugin looks like this:

```php
<?php
namespace Exam\Form\View\Helper\Question;

use Zend\Form\View\Helper\FormMultiCheckbox;
use Exam\Form\Element\Question\MultipleChoice;

class FormMultipleChoice extends FormMultiCheckbox {
  /**
   * Render options
   *
   * @param MultiCheckboxElement $element
   * @param array            $options
   * @param array            $selectedOptions
   * @param array            $attributes
   * @return string
   */
  protected function renderOptions(MultipleChoice $element, array $options,
                          array $selectedOptions, array $attributes)
  {
    $question = $element->getQuestion();
    $header  = $element->getHeader();

    $content = "<dd><pre>"
```

```
                . $this->getView()->escapeHtml($question)
                . "</pre></dd>";
        $content .= "<dl>$header</dl>";
        $content .= parent::renderOptions($element, $options,
                        $selectedOptions, $attributes);

        return $content;
    }
}
```

And the single choice is similar except that it extends from FormRadio:

```php
<?php
namespace Exam\Form\View\Helper\Question;
use Zend\Form\View\Helper\FormRadio;
use Exam\Form\Element\Question\SingleChoice;

class FormSingleChoice extends FormRadio
{
    /**
     * Render options
     *
     * @param MultiCheckboxElement $element
     * @param array           $options
     * @param array           $selectedOptions
     * @param array           $attributes
     * @return string
     */
    protected function renderOptions(SingleChoice $element,
                        array $options,
                        array $selectedOptions,
                        array $attributes)
    {
        $question = $element->getQuestion();
        $header  = $element->getHeader();

        $content  = "<dd><pre>"
            . $this->getView()->escapeHtml($question)
            . "</pre></dd>";
        $content .= "<dl>$header</dl>";
        $content .= parent::renderOptions($element, $options,
                        $selectedOptions, $attributes);

        return $content;
    }
}
```

In the **take.phtml** view template that will display the test, we need to use the custom *formQues-*

tionElement plugin to display form elements. The code below shows one way it can be used:

```php
<?php
$form->prepare();
echo $this->form()->openTag($form);
foreach ($form as $formElement) {
    if($formElement instanceof \Exam\Form\Element\Question\QuestionInterface) {
        echo $this->formQuestionElement($formElement);
    echo "<hr>\n";
    }
    else {
        echo $this->formRow($formElement);
    }
}


echo $this->form()->closeTag();
```

It is time to check what we have done up to this point. Make sure that you have the following route in your exam module configuration:

```php
'router' => array(
    'routes' => array(
        'exam' => array(
            'type'    => 'Literal',
            'options' => array(
                // Change this to something specific to your module
                'route'   => '/exam',
                'defaults' => array(
                    // Change this value to reflect the namespace in which
                    // the controllers for your module are found
                    '__NAMESPACE__' => 'Exam\Controller',
                    'controller'   => 'Test',
                    'action'       => 'index',
                ),
            ),
            'may_terminate' => true,
            'child_routes' => array(
                // This route is a sane default when developing a module;
                // as you solidify the routes for your module, however,
                // you may want to remove it and replace it with more
                // specific routes.
                'default' => array(
                    'type'    => 'Segment',
                    'options' => array(
                        'route'   => '/[:controller[/:action[/:id]]]',
                        'constraints' => array(
                            'controller' => '[a-zA-Z][a-zA-Z0-9_-]*',
```

```
            'action'   => '[a-zA-Z][a-zA-Z0-9_-]*',
            'id'       => '[0-9]*',
        ),
        'defaults' => array(
        ),
    ),
  ),
 ),
),
),
```

Once you have configured routing, type in your browser http://localhost/exam/test/take/1. If everything is fine you should see a page similar to the one below:

ZF2 Skeleton Application   Home ▾   User ▾

What is new in PHP 5.4

Only 1 of the following answers is correct.

○ namespaces
○ classes
○ traits
○ multiple inheritance

Which predifined constant will give you the current namespace?

Enter the answer in the text field

[   ]

```
What is the result from the following code?
<?php
$name="tAtIaNa";
```

If there are problems with this page either try to solve them yourself or, if you want to take the easy way, execute the commands below to get the source code:

```
cd <full/path/to/>/learnzf2/
git stash
git checkout 'ch-exam-take1'
```

Form Validation with Groups

For our test it is important to know how many questions were answered correctly. If we use the standard form verification in the *takeAction* we can be sure that 100% were answered correctly or an unknown percentage.

```php
public function takeAction()
{
    $id = $this->params('id');
    if(!$id) {
        return $this->redirect()->toRoute('exam/list);
    }

    $factory = new Factory();
    $spec = include __DIR__.'/../../../config/form/form1.php';
    $form = $factory->create($spec);

    $form->setAttribute('method', 'POST');

    $form->add(array(
                'type' => 'Zend\Form\Element\Csrf',
                'name' => 'security',
    ));

    $form->add(array(
                'type' => 'submit',
                'name' => 'submit',
                'attributes' => array (
                        'value' => 'Ready',
                )
    ));

    if ($this->getRequest()->isPost()) {
                $data = $this->getRequest()->getPost();
                $form->setData($data);
                $correct = 0;
                $total   = 0;
                if($form->isValid()) {
                    $this->flashmessenger()
            ->addSuccessMessage('Great! You have 100% correct answers.');

    //...
```

```
        ));

            }
            else {
                // @todo: Mark count the number of correct answers
            }

            return $this->redirect()->toRoute('exam/list');
    }

    // ..
    return array('form' => $form);
}
```

If we want to partially validate a form we can define validation groups in the form. We can also validate the question elements one by one. So the highlighted text from the code above can be replaced with the following code:

```
foreach ($form as $element) {
    if ($element instanceof QuestionInterface) {
        $total++;
        $form->setValidationGroup($element->getName());
        $form->setData($data);
        if ($form->isValid()) {
            $correct++;
        }
    }
}
```

In this manner we will be able to get the exact number of correct answers.

Test Questionnaires

We will create a reset action in the test controller that will fill the tests table with sample data. And we will improve the take action in the same controller. The table mysql definition should be saved under **module/Exam/sql/build.mysql.sql**. It looks like this:

```
DROP TABLE IF EXISTS tests;
CREATE TABLE tests (
        id integer(11) auto_increment primary key,
        name  varchar(255) NOT NULL,
        `locale` char(5) DEFAULT 'en_US',
        description TINYTEXT,
        duration smallint DEFAULT 60, -- the duration of the test in minutes
        creator integer(11),
        active boolean,
        definition text, -- serialized definition of test questions and answers
        cdate TIMESTAMP DEFAULT 0, -- created date
```

```
        mdate TIMESTAMP NULL ON UPDATE CURRENT_TIMESTAMP, -- modified date
        unique key(name,locale)
);
```

Test Manager

For managing the tests I will create a TestManager class that will be responsible for the following tasks:

1. Get the specification for the default sample tests
2. Build a form from a test specification
3. Get information about a test by *id*

The TestManager class should be saved as module/Exam/src/Model/TestManager.php. The initial code of this class is given below:

```php
<?php
namespace Exam\Model;

use Zend\ServiceManager\ServiceLocatorAwareInterface;
use Zend\ServiceManager\ServiceLocatorInterface;
use Zend\Form\Factory as FormFactory;

class TestManager implements ServiceLocatorAwareInterface
{
    /**
     * @var ServiceLocatorInterface
     */
    protected $services;

    /**
     * @var array
     */
    protected $cache;

    /**
     * Creates form for a  test
     * @param string $id
     * @return \Zend\Form\Form
     */
    public function createForm($id)
    {
        $data = $this->get($id);
        $spec = json_decode($data['definition'], true);
        if(!$spec) {
            throw new \Exception('Invalid form specification');
        }
```

```php
        $factory = new FormFactory();
        return $factory->create($spec);
    }

    public function get ($id)
    {
        if (! isset($this->cache[$id])) {
            // The Test class is a table gateway class
            $model = new Test();
            $result = $model->select(array('id' => $id));
                $data = $result->current();
                $this->cache[$id] = $data;
            }


        return $this->cache[$id];
    }

    public function store($data)
    {
        $model = new Test();
        return $model->insert($data);
    }



    /**
     * Gets data about the factory default tests
     *
     * @return array
     */
    public function getDefaultTests()
    {
            $formFiles = glob(__DIR__.'/../../../config/form/form*.php');
            $forms = array();
            foreach($formFiles as $file) {
                $forms[] = include_once $file;
            }

            return $forms;
    }
    // the setServiceLocator and getServiceLocator methods are skipped here
}
```

The TestManager relies on a Test *Table Gateway* class to communicate with the database. Be sure to add a Test *Table Gateway* class in your Exam module and save it as **module/Exam/src/ Exam/Model/Test.php**. The content of the Test.php class can look like this:

```php
<?php
namespace Exam\Model;
```

```php
use Zend\Db\TableGateway\AbstractTableGateway;
use Zend\Db\TableGateway\Feature;

class Test extends AbstractTableGateway
{
        public function __construct()
        {
                $this->table = 'tests';
                $this->featureSet = new Feature\FeatureSet();
                $this->featureSet->addFeature(new Feature\GlobalAdapterFeature());
                $this->initialize();
        }
}
```

Having a manager class helps us expose only the functionality that is safe for external modules to access, which allows us to limit access to the tests table. I will add TestManager registration in the service_manager => invokables module configuration key:

```php
'service_manager'=> array (
    //...
    'invokables' => array(
        'test-manager' => 'Exam\Model\TestManager',
        //...
    )
),
```

The *tests* table contains sensitive data. At the moment everyone who has access to the database can see the questions and their correct answers. Therefore we will use our cipher service to encrypt the data in the database. The improved TestManager looks like this:

```php
<?php
namespace Exam\Model;

//...

class TestManager implements ServiceLocatorAwareInterface
{
    //...
    public function get ($id)
    {
        if (! isset($this->cache[$id])) {
            $model = new Test();
            $result = $model->select(array('id' => $id));
            $data = $result->current();
            $data['definition'] = $this->services->get('cipher')->decrypt($data['definition']);
            $this->cache[$id] = $data;
        }
```

```php
        return $this->cache[$id];
    }

    public function store($data)
    {
        $model = new Test();
        $data['definition'] = $this->services->get('cipher')->encrypt($data['definition']);
        return $model->insert($data);
    }

    //...
}
```

Reset Action

Now we can code our *resetAction* method in the TestController:

```php
/**
 * Fills the tests with some default tests
 */
public function resetAction()
{
        $model = new Test();
        // delete all existing tests
        if($this->params('flush'))) {
           $model->delete(array());
        }

        // fill the default tests
        $manager = $this->serviceLocator->get('test-manager');
        $tests = $manager->getDefaultTests();
        foreach ($tests as $test) {
           $data = $test['info'];
           $data['definition'] = json_encode($test);
           $manager->store($data);
        }

        $this->flashmessenger()->addSuccessMessage('The default tests were added');
        return $this->redirect()->toRoute('exam/list');
}
```

Take Action

In the *take* action we can use the test manager to load a test from the database. We need to make the following change, highlighted below:

```php
public function takeAction()
{
        $id = $this->params('id');
```

```
if(!$id) {
      return $this->redirect()->toRoute('exam/list');
}

$testManager = $this->serviceLocator->get('test-manager');
$form = $testManager->createForm($id);

$form->setAttribute('method', 'POST');
```

Protecting and Adding Navigation to the Exam Actions

The *reset* action must be accessible to the admin user only. The *take* action should be accessible only from logged-in members. There will also be a third action that will list the available tests and will be visible to all users. The following needs to be added to the ACL definition in the Exam module:

```
'acl' => array(
      'resource' => array (
         'test' => null,
      ),
      'allow' => array(
         array('guest', 'test', 'list'),
         array('member', 'test', array('list','take')),
         array('admin', 'test', 'reset'),
      ),
      'modules' => array (
                     'Exam',
      ),
   ),
```

The following can be added to the module navigation configuration:

```
'navigation' => array(
      'default' => array(
         array(
            'label' => 'Exam',
            'route' => 'exam',
            'pages' => array(
               array(
                  'label' => 'List',
                  'route' => 'exam/list',
                  // acl
                  'resource'  => 'test',
                  'privilege'  => 'list',
               ),
               array(
                  'label' => 'Reset',
                  'title' => 'Resets the test to the default set',
```

```
                        // uri
                        'route' => 'exam/default',
                        'controller' => 'test',
                        'action'    => 'reset',
                        // acl
                        'resource'  => 'test',
                        'privilege' => 'reset',
                ),
            )
        ),
    )
),
```

Finally, we should add the *list* route to the Exam module:

```
'router' => array(
    'routes' => array(
        'exam' => array(
          'type'   => 'Literal',
          'options' => array(
            // Change this to something specific to your module
            'route'   => '/exam',
            'defaults' => array(
                // Change this value to reflect the namespace in which
                // the controllers for your module are found
                '__NAMESPACE__' => 'Exam\Controller',
                'controller'   => 'Test',
                'action'       => 'index',
            ),
          ),
          'may_terminate' => true,
          'child_routes' => array(
//..
              'list' => array(
                      'type'   => 'Literal',
                      'options' => array (
                              'route' => '/test/list',
                              'defaults' => array(
                                      'controller'  => 'Test',
                                      'action'      => 'list',
                                      ),
                              )
                      )
          ),
        ),
    ),
),
```

If you have an already existing user defined in the database, change his role to "admin" using your favorite database tool, and log in as this user. The *reset* and *list* menu items should show up under the Exam menu. Execute the reset and you will have the initial set of tests.

If there are problems with this page try to either solve them yourself or, if you want to go the easy way, execute the commands below to get the source code:

```
cd <full/path/to/>/learnzf2/
git stash
git checkout 'ch-exam-reset'
```

Pagination

Once we have tests in our database we have to list them somehow. For that reason we will implement the *list* action in the Test controller. The initial version of the list action gets information about all the tests and passes that information to the view:

```
use Exam\Model\Test;

// ...

public function listAction()
{
  $testModel = new Test();
  $result = $testModel->getSql()->select()->where(array('active'=> 1));

  return array('tests'=> $result);
}
```

As the number of tests increase, it will be better if we can limit the number of tests listed per page. For this purpose we can use the Zend\Paginator component. A *paginator* is designed to show a certain number of items per page as well as the total number of pages and items. This way we can have thousands of tests and not overwhelm our users.

Every paginator needs an adapter. The adapter represents a system that provides the source of the information we wish to display. In our case we will use the database page adapter. This adapter accepts an SQL query that will be used to fetch the appropriate data set. An initial query, executed once, counts the total number of items. A second query retrieves only the items that are within the current page range. After some modifications the *listAction* method looks like this:

```
use Zend\Paginator\Adapter\DbSelect as PaginatorDbAdapter;
use Zend\Paginator\Paginator;

// ..

public function listAction()
{
    $testModel = new Test();
    $result = $testModel->getSql()->select()->where(array('active'=> 1));

    $adapter = new PaginatorDbAdapter($result, $testModel->getAdapter());
    $paginator = new Paginator($adapter);

    return array('tests'=> $paginator);
}
```

We must also specify the current page and the number of items per page:

```php
public function listAction()
{
    $testModel = new Test();
    $result = $testModel->getSql()->select()->where(array('active'=> 1));

    $adapter = new PaginatorDbAdapter($result, $testModel->getAdapter());
    $paginator = new Paginator($adapter);
    $currentPage = $this->params('page', 1);
    $paginator->setCurrentPageNumber($currentPage);
    $paginator->setItemCountPerPage(10);

    return array('tests'=> $paginator,
                 'page'=> $currentPage
        );
}
```

In the code above we get the current page from the *page* parameter. By using the *params* plugin directly we can acquire the page number regardless of whether it is coming from the route match, or as a *get* or *post* parameter.

The paginator has view plugins that help us display the content. The **list.phtml** view has the following code:

```php
<?php if (count($this->tests)): ?>

<table class="table table-striped">
<thead>
  <tr>
    <th><?= $this->translate('Name') ?></th>
    <th><?= $this->translate('Description') ?></th>
    <th><?= $this->translate('Duration') ?></th>
    <th></th>
    <th></th>
    <th></th>
  </tr>
</thead>
<tbody>
<?php foreach ($this->tests as $test): ?>
  <!-- Iterate over the tests and show the information about them -->
<?php endforeach; ?>
</tbody>
</table>
<?php endif; ?>


<?php echo $this->paginationControl($this->tests,
                'Sliding',
                'paginator/sliding',
```

```
                    array('route' => 'exam/list')
                    );
```

In the code shown above, the *paginationControl* view plugin is the important thing to note. It takes as a first argument the paginator instance. After that we can specify the style in which we want the list of pages to be shown, followed by the fully qualified name of the view template that will be used to display the actual paging data. The last argument is the route that will be used to render the links when you click on a certain page number.

In the example above, the view template and routing parameters are the ones that require our attention. In our application we can add the view template description to the Application module and place there the actual view code. The Application module configuration will have the highlighted lines below.

```
'view_manager' => array(
    // ...
    'exception_template'    => 'error/index',
    'template_map' => array(
      'error/index'        => __DIR__ . '/../view/error/index.phtml',
      // paginator views
      'paginator/sliding'    => __DIR__ . '/../view/paginator/sliding.phtml',
    ),
    'template_path_stack' => array(
      __DIR__ . '/../view',
    ),
  ),
```

The view template code will be saved as **module/Application/view/paginator/sliding.phtml** and can have the following content:

```php
<!--
See http://developer.yahoo.com/ypatterns/pattern.php?pattern=itempagination
-->

<?php if ($this->pageCount): ?>
<div class="paginationControl">
<?php echo $this->firstItemNumber; ?> - <?php echo $this->lastItemNumber; ?>
of <?php echo $this->totalItemCount; ?>

<!-- First page link -->
<?php if (isset($this->previous)): ?>
  <a href="<?php echo $this->url($this->route, array('page' => $this->first)); ?>">
    First
  </a> |
<?php else: ?>
  <span class="disabled">First</span> |
<?php endif; ?>

<!-- Previous page link -->
<?php if (isset($this->previous)): ?>
```

```
<a href="<?php echo $this->url($this->route, array('page' => $this->previous)); ?>">
  < Previous
</a> |
<?php else: ?>
<span class="disabled">< Previous</span> |
<?php endif; ?>

<!-- Next page link -->
<?php if (isset($this->next)): ?>
  <a href="<?php echo $this->url($this->route, array('page' => $this->next)); ?>">
  Next >
  </a> |
<?php else: ?>
  <span class="disabled">Next ></span> |
<?php endif; ?>

<!-- Last page link -->
<?php if (isset($this->next)): ?>
  <a href="<?php echo $this->url($this->route, array('page' => $this->last)); ?>">
  Last
  </a>
<?php else: ?>
  <span class="disabled">Last</span>
<?php endif; ?>

</div>
<?php endif; ?>
```

The highlighted text shows the name of the parameter that we will use to specify the current page.

The view template parameter and its associated code was our first consideration. The second is to define a configuration key to match the routing parameter. In the Exam module configuration, we need to add the exam/list route that defines the page parameter, which must be valid number. This can be described using constraints. Our routing table will have the following new definition:

```
return array(
   'router' => array(
     'routes' => array(
       'exam' => array(
         'type'   => 'Literal',
         'options' => array(
           'route'  => '/exam',
           'defaults' => array(
             '__NAMESPACE__' => 'Exam\Controller',
             'controller'  => 'Index',
             'action'    => 'index',
           ),
```

```php
            ),
            'may_terminate' => true,
            'child_routes' => array(
                'default' => array(
                    // ...
                ),
                'list' => array(
                    'type'    => 'Segment',
                    'options' => array(
                        'route'   => '/test/list[/:page]',
                        'constraints' => array(
                            'page'    => '[0-9]*',
                        ),
                        'defaults' => array(
                            'controller'=> 'test',
                            'action'   => 'list',
                            'page'              => 1,
                        ),
                    ),
                )
            ),
        ),
    ),
),
```

The *list* view will need to have information about the currently logged-in user and access control lists. We could pass the user object directly from the action to the view. On the other hand, if we want to have a more generic solution, we can modify the User module to have the current user object injected into the view model when we start rendering data. The same solution will be applied to the ACL. The following changes are needed in **module/User/Module.php**:

```php
public function onBootstrap(MvcEvent $event)
{
        //...
        $eventManager->attach('render', array($this, 'injectUserAcl'));
}
//...
public function injectUserAcl(MvcEvent $event)
{
        if(!$event->getResponse()->contentSent()) {
                $services = $event->getApplication()->getServiceManager();
                $viewModel = $event->getResult();
                if($viewModel instanceof ViewModel) {
                        $viewModel->setVariable('user', $services->get('user'));
                        $viewModel->setVariable('acl', $services->get('acl'));
                }
        }
},
```

Now open in your web browser to http://localhost/exam/test/list, and check whether you can see the available tests. If you did not disable the Debug module you can see the SQL queries executed and the time elapsed.

If there are problems with this page, try to either solve them yourself, or, if you want to go the easy route, execute the commands below to get the source code:

```
cd <full/path/to/>/learnzf2/
git stash
git checkout 'ch-pagination'
```

Better Performance

In this chapter I will show you how you can improve the performance of our ZF2 application. The Debug module calculates the time a request is taking. Before we start lets check how long it takes to load the list of tests. Take a look at the PHP error log to see the time for this request. On my old computer it takes roughly 43 ms to render the page. Let's see if we can decrease that time.

Speeding up ZF2 Module Loading

On every request ZF2 has to load and merge together the configuration from all enabled modules. This is time consuming and, in a production environment, is unnecessary effort as most of the time the configuration does not change at all. Additionally, if the classes that we load are not in the class map, the autoloaders would have to find them, taking extra time.

In ZF2 you can quite easily cache this information. The correct place to specify these settings is in the application configuration under the *module_listener_options* key. Let's add the following code to our application config file:

```php
return array(
   'modules' => array(
     'Application',
     'Debug',
     'User',
     'Exam'
   ),
   'module_listener_options' => array(
     'config_glob_paths'   => array(
       'config/autoload/{,*.}{global,local}.php',
     ),
     'module_paths' => array(
       './module',
       './vendor',
     ),

     // Whether or not to enable a configuration cache.
     // If enabled, the merged configuration will be cached and used in
     // subsequent requests.
     'config_cache_enabled' => true,
     // The key used to create the configuration cache file name.
     'config_cache_key' => "1",

     // Whether or not to enable a module class map cache.
     // If enabled, creates a module class map cache which will be used
     // by in future requests, to reduce the autoloading process.
     'module_map_cache_enabled' => true,
     // The key used to create the class map cache file name.
     'module_map_cache_key' => "1",
```

```
    // The path in which to cache merged configuration.
    'cache_dir' => "data/cache/module",
  ),
);
```

In order to test this configuration we also need to create the **cache/module** directory under **<full/path/to/>/learnzf2/data**.

```
cd <full/path/to/>/learnzf2
mkdir -p data/cache/module
```

You will also need to make this directory writable, executable and readable for the web server user (the user account under which the web server is running). In my case the web server user is **www-data**. Don't make it readable for other users or groups as your configuration may contain sensitive information.

```
cd data/
chown www-data:www-data -R cache/module/
chmod 0700 cache/module
```

Once you have completed the creation of the cache folder, let's check if there is an improvement in application speed. Load the list page at least two times and take a look at the MVC execution time information from the Debug module. In my case, after checking both requests, I noticed the time was reduced to 30 ms. This is not bad at all!

> **Notice**
>
> In the cache directory there should be a new file created called module-config-cache.1.php. This file contains the final application configuration. You can check if it contains the data that you were expecting.

What we need to remember is that as we continue to develop our application, any changes to application or module configuration will not be reflected in cache. This means we need to either disable the cache, or change the values for module and config cache keys from the application configuration, every time we change module configuration or refactor our classes.

This is a problem! One elegant solution to this problem is to make the cache directory on your development machine, and only on that one machine, not readable and writable for the web server user. When you have finished your changes and want to restore caching, make the cache directory again readable and writable.

Class and Template Maps

Loading class and template files using the class map autoloader can give you an additional performance boost. The class map is an associative array where the key is the name of the class (or template), and the value is the full path to the physical file which represents the class or template. Trying to load a class or template using class maps is done using fast array lookup.

In order to generate a class map or template map in ZF2, there are two scripts you can use: **classmap_generator.php** and **templatemap_generator.php** respectively. They are located in the **bin** directory of the ZF2 installation. When it is time to release a new version and deploy it on the server, you can run these two scripts for each module to improve performance.

In order for the application to use the class map you need to make sure that you are using the *class map autoloader*. Open the **Module.php** file and check if the highlighted code is present. If not add the code highlighted below:

```php
public function getAutoloaderConfig()
{
    return array(
        'Zend\Loader\ClassMapAutoloader' => array(
            __DIR__ . '/autoload_classmap.php',
        ),
        'Zend\Loader\StandardAutoloader' => array(
            'namespaces' => array(
                // if we're in a namespace deeper than one level we need to fix the \ in the path
                __NAMESPACE__ => __DIR__ . '/src/' . str_replace('\\', '/' , __NAMESPACE__),
            ),
        ),
    );
}
```

To take advantage of the template map you have to change your **module.config.php** file to contain the following configuration information:

```php
'view_manager' => array(
    'template_path_stack' => array(
        __DIR__ . '/../view',
    ),
    'template_map' => include __DIR__ . '/../template_map.php',
),
```

We will add these maps to our User module for a demonstration. Creating a class map can be accomplished with the following command:

```
cd module/User/
php ../../vendor/zendframework/zendframework/bin/classmap_generator.php
```

You can create a template map with a similar command:

```
cd module/User/
php ../../vendor/zendframework/zendframework/bin/templatemap_generator.php
```

Cache

Enabling Cache

In some cases the generation of data takes time and resources. Caching can improve the performance of our application in such cases, using the ZF2 Zend\Cache component. The easiest way to enable cache is to register a cache service. A caching service can be useful for the complete application therefore we will register it in the Application module config:

```
'service_manager'=> array (
        'factories'  => array(
            // ...
              'text-cache' => 'Zend\Cache\Service\StorageCacheFactory',
        ),
    //
    ),
```

The cache configuration is varies depending on the application environment. You should there-fore save such configuration in the **module/Application/config/cache.local.php.dist** file. One example of such configuration is shown below:

```
<?php
return array(
// Cache that is used only for storing and fetching data without
// any form of convertion.
  'cache' => array (
    'adapter' => array(
      'name' => 'filesystem',
      'options' => array (
        'cache_dir' => 'data/cache/text',
      )
    ),
    'plugins' => array(
      // Don't throw exceptions on cache errors
      'exception_handler' => array(
        'throw_exceptions' => false
      ),
      //...
    )
  ),
);
```

And in order to use the configuration we have to copy the ".dist" file to the application config directory, and save it as **<full/path/to/>/learnzf2/config/autoload/cache.local.php**.

The cache configuration contains an **adapter** key, which specifies the actual system that will physically store the cached data. Under the **adapter** key we have two subkeys: name and op-tions. In ZF2, at the moment of this writing, you can store cache on the file system, in memory using Memcached, Zend Server, APC (Alternative PHP Cache), among other caching systems. The complete list of cache adapters can be found in the ZF2 website[40].

Another configuration key allows you to define cache *plugins*[41] that add functionality, change or improve the behavior of the cache system. In our case we specified not to throw exceptions if the cache system is not able to store or fetch data.

Cache Profiling

Now we are ready to use cache. For a cache system it is important to have more hits than misses.

---

40 http://framework.zend.com/manual/2.1/en/modules/zend.cache.storage.adapter.html
41 http://framework.zend.com/manual/2.1/en/modules/zend.cache.storage.plugin.html

A *hit* is when information was successfully read from cache. A *miss* means that the information was not present in cache when needed.

As developers it is important to have an idea what is going on with our cache. That is why we will add code in our Debug module that allows us to track cache hits and misses. I will add an *initializer* in the Debug module that will allow us to do so. The initializer code, saved as **module/Debug/Initializer/CacheProfiler.php** can look like:

```php
<?php
namespace Debug\Service\Initializer;

use Zend\Cache\Storage\Event;
use Zend\Cache\Storage\StorageInterface;
use Zend\Cache\Storage\PostEvent;
use Zend\ServiceManager\InitializerInterface;
use Zend\ServiceManager\ServiceLocatorInterface;

class CacheProfiler implements InitializerInterface
{
    /**
     * Initialize
     *
     * @param $instance
     * @param ServiceLocatorInterface $serviceLocator
     * @return mixed
     */
    public function initialize($instance, ServiceLocatorInterface $serviceLocator)
    {
            if ($instance instanceof StorageInterface) {
            // @todo:...
        }
    }
}
```

The cache service has its own event manager and we can attach listeners that hook to events which are of interest to us. The **getItem.pre** event is triggered before the cache backend adapter provides the cached data for a special key. The **getItem.post event** is triggered when the cache backend has answered the request.

We will attach our own listeners that count the hits. If the returned data for the **getItem.post** event is null this means that we have cache miss. Otherwise, we will count it as cache hit. Let's see how this can be implemented in our initializer:

```php
<?php
namespace Debug\Service\Initializer;

use Zend\Cache\Storage\Event;
use Zend\Cache\Storage\StorageInterface;
use Zend\Cache\Storage\PostEvent;
use Zend\ServiceManager\InitializerInterface;
use Zend\ServiceManager\ServiceLocatorInterface;
```

```php
class CacheProfiler implements InitializerInterface
{
    /**
     * @var \stdClass
     */
    protected $stats;

    /**
     * @var ServiceLocatorInterface
     */
    protected $services;

    /**
     * Initialize
     *
     * @param $instance
     * @param ServiceLocatorInterface $serviceLocator
     * @return mixed
     */
    public function initialize($instance, ServiceLocatorInterface $serviceLocator)
    {
        if ($instance instanceof StorageInterface) {
            // Every cache service has its own event manager
            $cacheEventManager = $instance->getEventManager();
            // And we can listen to getItem.pre and getItem.post events
            // to find out if we have cache hit or cache miss.
            $cacheEventManager->attach('getItem.pre' ,array($this, 'preGetCache'));
            $cacheEventManager->attach('getItem.post',array($this,'postGetCache'));
            if(!$this->stats) {
                // Because we want to be able to access the counter from the Module class
                // we can store the information into a service called cache-profiler
                $stats = new \stdClass();
                $stats->hits = array();
                $serviceLocator->setService('cache-profiler', $stats);
                $this->stats = $stats;
                $this->services = $serviceLocator;
            }
        }
    }

    public function preGetCache(Event $event)
    {
        $key = $event->getParam('key');
        if(!isset($this->stats->hits[$key])) {
            $this->stats->hits[$key] = 0;
        }
```

```
        }

        public function postGetCache(PostEvent $event)
        {
            $key = $event->getParam('key');
            if(null !== $event->getResult()) {
                    // if we have a hit we increment the counter
                    $this->stats->hits[$key]++;
            }
        }
}
```

Do not forget to register this *initializer* in the Debug module configuration.

In order to display this information in the debug layout we can inject it into the view from the *injectViewVariables* method in the **Module.php** file:

```
/**
    * Injects common variables in the view model
    * @param MvcEvent $event
    */
   public function injectViewVariables(MvcEvent $event)
   {
       $viewModel = $event->getViewModel();

       $services = $event->getApplication()->getServiceManager();
       $variables = array();
       //..

       if($services->has('cache-profiler')){
          $variables['cache'] = $services->get('cache-profiler');
       };

       if(!empty($variables)) {
          $viewModel->setVariables($variables);
       }
   }
```

Finally, we will have to add code that displays cache hits in the **debug/layout/sidebar.phtml** view template:

```
if ($this->profiler) {
   // ..
}

echo '<div id="cache">Cache Hits:';
foreach($this->cache->hits as $key=>$count) {
        echo "$key => $count<br>\n";
}
```

```
echo '</div>';
?>
```

That will be enough to track hits. If you also want to track the time that a cache request takes to complete, then you can improve the *preGetCache* and *postGetCache* methods from the Cache-Profiler initializer.

Using Cache

The two most important methods when working with cache are *getItem($key)* and *setItem($key, $valueToCache)*. For those of you that have already used caching under PHP it may seem like something is missing. The usual expiration date, also known as Time To Live (TTL), cannot be specified per cached item. In ZF2 the TTL can be specified for the cache instance as a whole using the cache option *ttl*.

```php
<?php
return array(
  'cache' => array (
    'adapter' => array(
      'name' => 'filesystem',
      'options' => array (
        'cache_dir' => 'data/cache',
        'ttl'     => 100,
      )
    ),
    'plugins' => array(
      // ...
    )
  ),
);
```

It is also possible to perform the following operations:

Operation	Zend\Cache\Storage\Adapter Method
Check for the existence of a key	*hasItem($key)*
Increment an item key value	*incrementItem($key)*
Decrement key value	*decrementItem($key)*
Replace	*replaceItem($key, $newValue)*
Remove	*removeItem($key)*

Note that each of these operations triggers a *.pre and *.post event (i.e. *hasItem.pre, hasItem. post, incrementItem.pre, incrementItem.post*, etc.).

In the discussion which follows, you will see how we can use the cache for some ZF2 components that were already mentioned in this book.

Caching Parts of the Code

The pagination is making two SQL requests to get the data. At the moment they take very little time to execute, but as the table grows in size, the time to execute SQL requests will increase.

Therefore, it makes sense to cache this data. In order to use cache in the paginator, following the ZF2 Reference Guide, we should make these changes in the Exam module's TestController *listAction*:

```php
public function listAction()
{
    $testModel = new Test();
    $result = $testModel->getSql()->select()->where(array('active'=> 1));

    $adapter = new PaginatorDbAdapter($result, $testModel->getAdapter());
    $paginator = new Paginator($adapter);

    $cache = $this->serviceLocator->get('cache');
    \Zend\Paginator\Paginator::setCache($cache);

    $paginator->setCacheEnabled(true); // just in case the cache was disabled

    // ...
}
```

Unfortunately, at the time of this writing, this feature is not working. How do I know? The Debug module we have been discussing in this book reported only cache misses, and different cache keys are being loaded on every page request! In addition, the SQL profiler showed that two SQL requests were executed each time. On the one hand this is bad news. On the other hand this is a great opportunity to demonstrate how we can cache.

The general procedure for using cache is as follows:
- Specify a unique key when caching the data
- Check if there is data in the cache
- If not, proceed with the core logic and save the generated data into cache

In the *list* action we can have the following code:

```php
public function listAction()
{
    $currentPage = $this->params('page', 1);
    $cacheKey = 'exam-list-'.$currentPage;

    // Non-core logic to check if we have the data in cache alread
    $cache = $this->serviceLocator->get('var-cache');
    $paginator = $cache->getItem($cacheKey);

    if (!$paginator) {
        // Core Logic related to listing tests
        $testModel = new Test();
        $result = $testModel->getSql()->select()->where(array('active'=> 1));

        $adapter = new PaginatorDbAdapter($result, $testModel->getAdapter());
        $paginator = new Paginator($adapter);
```

```
        $paginator->setCurrentPageNumber($currentPage);
        $paginator->setItemCountPerPage(10);

        // Non-Core to save the data in the cache
        $cache->setItem($cache, $paginator->toArray());
    }
```

Although the code shown above allows us to use cache, there is now caching code which is not part of the core logic. Additionally, if we want to add caching to other actions, we would have to repeat the same cache code again and again. In the next sections I will show you how we can provide a better soltuion using *Full Page Caching* or *Action Caching*.

Full Page Caching

In ZF2 we can cache the complete HTML output. This technique is known as *full page caching*. To accomplish this, we can attach a listener to an event that is triggered after routing, to activate full page cache. Another listener will be executed by an event which is triggered long after rendering, which can then save output to cache. We will add these changes to the **module/Application/Module.php** file. The initial version of the *onBootstap* method can look like this:

```
public function onBootstrap(MvcEvent $e)
{
    $services = $e->getApplication()->getServiceManager();
    //...

    if($services->has('text-cache')) {
        // This will be used to check if there is already cached page and return it.
        // The priority must be low in order to be executed after the routing is done
    $eventManager->attach(MvcEvent::EVENT_ROUTE, array($this,'getPageCache'), -1000);
        // And this will be used to save a generated cache page.
        // The priority must be low in order to be executed after rendering is done
    $eventManager->attach(MvcEvent::EVENT_RENDER,
            array($this,'savePageCache'), -10000);
    }
}
```

Notice that the listeners are attached with a very low priority so that they are triggered after routing and rendering is finished.

If we want to be able to specify which page to cache, and not blindly cache all pages, in the routing table we can add a parameter *pagecache.* If we want to cache the complete exam list page then we should edit the Exam module configuration and make the following change:

```
return array(
    'router' => array(
        'routes' => array(
            'exam' => array(
                //...
                'may_terminate' => true,
                'child_routes' => array(
```

```
        // ...
     'list' => array(
                         'type'   => 'Segment',
                         'options' => array(
                                       'route'   => '/test/list[/:page]',
                                       'constraints' => array(
                                               'page'    => '[0-9]*',
                                       ),
                                       'defaults' => array(
                                               'controller'=> 'test',
                                               'action'   => 'list',
                                               'page'                => 1,
                                               'pagecache' => true,
                                       ),
                         ),
         )
       ),
     ),
   ),
  ),
//...
```

The name of the parameter can be changed to something else, if appropriate. You just need to set a strict rule when coding how to name it so that the event listeners will understand when a page should be cached.

Let's go back to the **module/Application/Module.php** file and add the post route listener:

```php
public function getPageCache(MvcEvent $event)
{
    $match = $event->getRouteMatch();
    if(!$match) {
        return;
    }

    if($match->getParam('pagecache')) {
        // the page can be cached so lets check if we have a cache copy of it
      $cache = $event->getApplication()
            ->getServiceManager()
            ->get('text-cache');
      $cacheKey = $this->pageCacheKey($match);
      $data = $cache->getItem($cacheKey);
      if(null !== $data) {
        $response = $event->getResponse();
        $response->setContent($data);

        // When we return a response object we actually shortcut execution:
        // the action responsible for this page is not executed
        return $response;
```

```
        }
    }
}
```

The code that saves the rendered content can look like this:

```
public function savePageCache(MvcEvent $event)
  {
     $match = $event->getRouteMatch();
     if(!$match) {
         return;
     }

     if($match->getParam('pagecache')) {
        $response = $event->getResponse();
        $data = $response->getContent();
        $cache = $event->getApplication()
                ->getServiceManager()
                ->get('text-cache');
        $cacheKey = $this->pageCacheKey($match);
        $cache->setItem($cacheKey, $data);
     }
  }
```

What is missing is the generation of the cache key. As a start we can use the following method:

```
 /**
  * Generates valid page cache key
  *
  * @param RouteMatch $match
  * @return string
  */
 protected function pageCacheKey(RouteMatch $match)
 {
         return 'pagecache_'
                 . str_replace('/', '-', $match->getMatchedRouteName())
                 . '_'
                 . md5(serialize($match->getParams()));
 }
```

Let's say you have different translations for your website. And if you want to deliver the French version to a French speaking user, you have to somehow distinguish this from the German or English version. One easy solution, if the current language value is kept in a cookie named *LANG*, is to change the routing definition, and as a value for the *pagecache* parameter assign **$_COOKIE['LANG']**.

```
  'list' => array(
        'type'  => 'Segment',
```

```
'options' => array(
  'route'  => '/test/list[/:page]',
  'constraints' => array(
          'page'  => '[0-9]*',
  ),
  'defaults' => array(
          'controller'=> 'test',
          'action'  => 'list',
          'page'          => 1,
          'pagecache' => isset($_COOKIE['LANG'])
                  ? $_COOKIE['LANG'] : 'en',
  ),
 ),
),
```

Notice that the page cache will include the entire layout. This includes the navigation, which is different for every user role. In that case you should also think about adding role based rule checking into the cache key. Another solution will be to cache only the content from the action and exclude the layout.

Action Cache

More often it makes sense to cache only the content that should be produced from the action, excluding any layout or debug information. Action caching can be more complex than page caching. There are two steps required to achieve this:

Step	Action	Notes
1	Getting Cache	For this step we need to add a listener to an event that is triggered before the actual action, and check if there is cache data. If so, we need to create a new *View Model* and inject any pure text data.
2	Saving Cache	In order to save cache we need to get the result from the action and transform it into text. We will need a listener attached to an event that is triggered when rendering starts. Since we are getting back PHP variables there are cases where these variables cannot be presented as text. One example would be a result set obtained from a database. This means that we have to either always try to return from our actions data that can be represented as text, which will make our core code very ugly, or just try to render the result and save the rendered text. I will use the second approach.

I created the following methods and listeners to allow our application to save only the action cache. All changes are made in **module/Application/Module.php**:

```php
<?php
/**
 * Zend Framework (http://framework.zend.com/)
 *
 * @link        http://github.com/zendframework/ZendSkeletonApplication for the canonical
 * source repository
 * @copyright Copyright (c) 2005-2012 Zend Technologies USA Inc. (http://www.zend.com)
 * @license   http://framework.zend.com/license/new-bsd New BSD License
```

```php
*/

namespace Application;

use Zend\Mvc\ModuleRouteListener;
use Zend\Mvc\MvcEvent;
use Zend\Mvc\Router\RouteMatch;
use Zend\View\Model\ViewModel;

class Module
{
  public function onBootstrap(MvcEvent $e)
  {
    //..

    $services = $e->getApplication()->getServiceManager();
    if($services->has('text-cache')) {
      // ...
      $eventManager->attach(MvcEvent::EVENT_DISPATCH,
              array($this,'getActionCache'), 2);
      $eventManager->attach(MvcEvent::EVENT_RENDER,
              array($this,'saveActionCache'), 0);
    }

    //...
  }


  // Action cache implementation
  public function getActionCache(MvcEvent $event)
  {
    $match = $event->getRouteMatch();
    if(!$match) {
      return;
    }

    if($match->getParam('actioncache')) {
      $cache = $event->getApplication()
            ->getServiceManager()
            ->get('text-cache');
      $cacheKey = $this->actionCacheKey($match);
      $data = $cache->getItem($cacheKey);
      if(null !== $data) {
        // When data comes from the cache
        // we don't want the saveActionCache method to refresh this cache
        $match->setParam('actioncache',false);
```

```php
        $viewModel = $event->getViewModel();
        $viewModel->setVariable($viewModel->captureTo(), $data);
        $event->stopPropagation(true);
        return $viewModel;
      }
   }
}

public function saveActionCache(MvcEvent $event)
{
   $match = $event->getRouteMatch();
   if(!$match) {
      return;
   }

   if($match->getParam('actioncache')) {
      $viewManager = $event->getApplication()
                ->getServiceManager()
                ->get('viewmanager');

      $result   = $event->getResult();
      if($result instanceof ViewModel) {
         $cache = $event->getApplication()
                ->getServiceManager()
                ->get('text-cache');
         // Warning: The line below needs improvement.
         // It will work for all PHP templates, but would have
         // to be made more flexible if you had planned to use
         // other template systems.
         $renderer = $viewManager->getRenderer();

         $content = $renderer->render($result);
         $cacheKey = $this->actionCacheKey($match);
         $cache->setItem($cacheKey, $content);
         $tags = $match->getParam('tags');
         if (is_array($tags)) {
            $cache->setTags($cacheKey, $tags);
         }
      }
   }
}

/**
 * Generates valid page cache key
 *
 * @param RouteMatch $match
```

```
 * @param string $prefix
 * @return string
 */
protected function pageCacheKey(RouteMatch $match, $prefix='pagecache_')
{
   return  $prefix.str_replace('/', '-',
                  $match->getMatchedRouteName())
              .'_'. md5(serialize($match->getParams()));
}

/**
 * Generates valid action cache key
 *
 * @param RouteMatch $match
 * @param string $prefix
 * @return string
 */
protected function actionCacheKey(RouteMatch $match, $prefix='actioncache_')
{
   return $this->pageCacheKey($match, $prefix);
}
}
```

I will also change the Exam module Test controller *list* action to use only action cache:

```
'list' => array(
              'type'    => ,Segment',
              'options' => array (
                'route' => ,/test/list[/:page]',
                'constraints' => array(
                   'page'    => ,[0-9]*',
                ),
                'defaults' => array(
                   'controller'  => ,Test',
                   'action'      => ,list',
                   'page'        => ,1',
                   // 'pagecache'  => true,
                   'actioncache'  => true,
//...
)
```

Serializers

By default cache data is stored without any transformation. This means that when we try to store PHP data types other than simple scalars (i.e. string, int, float, boolean) into our cache, it most certainly won't work! In order to be able to store these complex data types we need to enable a *serializer* for our cache.

"... Serialization is the process of translating data structures or object state into a format that can be

stored (for example, in a file or memory buffer, or transmitted across a network connection link) and "resurrected" later in the same or another computer environment ..."[42]

Serialization and de-serialization takes time and resources. Therefore we must choose our serializer wisely. ZF2 provides a good range of serializers[43]. Some of them allow the serialized data to be exchanged between applications written in different languages: *WDDX*, *PythonPickle* and *JSON*. Other serializers provide text representation that can be used only from PHP: *PhpSerialize* and *PhpCode*. And finally there is the binary PHP only representation *IgBinary*. For our example we will use *PhpSerialize*.

It will be better in our application to have two cache services. One will not have a serializer, and will store and read data without conversion. The second one will have a serializer. We already have the first cache service defined and running. For the second one, we need to add the configuration shown below:

```php
<?php
return array(
    // Cache that is used only for storing and fetching data without convertion
    'cache' => array(
        // ...
    ),
    // Variables cache that serializes the data when storing it and unserializes it when reading it
    'var-cache' => array (
        'adapter' => array(
            'name' => 'filesystem',
            'options' => array (
                'cache_dir' => 'data/cache/var',
            )
        ),
        'plugins' => array(
            // Don't throw exceptions on cache errors
            'exception_handler' => array(
                'throw_exceptions' => false
            ),
            'serializer' => array (
                'serializer' => 'Zend\Serializer\Adapter\PhpSerialize',
            )
        )
    ),
);
```

And we will register a new *var-cache* service that uses this configuration.

```php
'service_manager'=> array (
        'factories'  => array(
                // ...
                'text-cache'    => 'Zend\Cache\Service\StorageCacheFactory',
                'var-cache'     => 'Application\Service\Factory\VariableCache',
```

42 http://en.wikipedia.org/wiki/Serialization
43 http://framework.zend.com/manual/2.1/en/modules/zend.serializer.html

```
        ),
        'invokables' => array(
        //...
    )
),
```

The code for the service looks like this:

```php
<?php
namespace Application\Service\Factory;

use Zend\ServiceManager\FactoryInterface;
use Zend\ServiceManager\ServiceLocatorInterface;
use Zend\Cache\StorageFactory;

class VariableCache implements FactoryInterface
{
        /* (non-PHPdoc)
         * @see \Zend\ServiceManager\FactoryInterface::createService()
         */
        public function createService(ServiceLocatorInterface $serviceLocator)
        {
                $config = $serviceLocator->get('config');
                $cache = StorageFactory::factory($config['var-cache']);
                return $cache;
        }
}
```

The new variable cache service can be used to cache translations. In the **cache.local.php*** file we can add the following lines:

```php
'cache-enabled-services' => array(
        'translator',
),
```

The configuration above will allow us to enable or disable cache for these services. The lines of code shown below demonstrate how to activate cache in a specific class without the need of having it available as a service.

```php
'cache-enabled-classes' => array(
        ' \\Zend\\Paginator\\Paginator',
)
```

We can also control the settings for different application environments.

In the Application module **Module.php** file, we can add the following code that automates variable cache enabling for these services:

```
public function onBootstrap(MvcEvent $e)
{
    $services = $e->getApplication()->getServiceManager();
    //...

    if($services->has('var-cache')) {
      $config = $services->get('config');
      $cache  = $services->get('var-cache');

      // Enables cache for services
      if(isset($config['cache-enabled-services'])) {
        foreach($config['cache-enabled-services'] as $serviceName) {
          if($services->has($serviceName)) {
            $services->get($serviceName)->setCache($cache);
          }
        }
      }

      // Enables cache for classes
      if(isset($config['cache-enabled-classes'])) {
        foreach($config['cache-enabled-classes'] as $className) {
                call_user_func($className.'::setCache', $cache);
        }
      }
    }
}
```

Logically Grouping Keys

Some of the cache adapters allow us to logically group cache keys. In ZF2 there are two possible ways to group them. The first is by using a namespace prefix when adding a key. For this to work the cache adapter must implement the interface **Zend\Cache\Storage\ClearByNamespaceInterface.** Sample usage is given below:

```
$cache = $this->serviceLocator->get('cache');
// storing data
$cache->setItem('paginator:page1', $value1);
$cache->setItem('paginator:page2', $value2);

// clearing all keys in the namespace can be done with the following code
if ($cache instanceof \Zend\Cache\Storage\ClearByNamespaceInterface) {
    $cache->clearByNamespace('paginator');
}
```

The second way to logically group keys is to tag them. This is more flexible than namespacing the key because you can have multiple tags for a single key. For this to work the cache adapter has to implement **Zend\Cache\Storage\TaggableInterface.** Sample usage is given below:

```php
$cache = $this->serviceLocator->get('cache');
// we store two keys and attach tags to them
if($cache->setItem('page1', $value1)) {
   $cache->setTags('page1', array('pagination','exams'));
}
if($cache->setItem('page2', $value1)) {
      $cache->setTags('page2', array('pagination'));
}

// Below we clear all keys that have tag exam.
// This example clears only cache key "page1".
if ($cache instanceof \Zend\Cache\Storage\TaggableInterface) {
   $cache->clearByTags(array('exam'));
}
```

Now let's apply this functionality to our Exam module. The *resetAction* in the TestController will have the following change:

```php
/**
 * Fills the tests with some default tests
 */
public function resetAction()
{
      // ..
      $cache = $this->serviceLocator->get('text-cache');
      $cache->clearByTags(array('exam-list'));

      //...

      $this->flashmessenger()->addSuccessMessage('The default tests were added');
      return $this->redirect()->toRoute('exam/list');
}
```

Cache cleaning will work quite nicely if we do not have page cache or action cache enabled. If we want to improve our page and action cache, we can add a *tags* key to the routing definition. The routing for the *list* action will have the following change in the **module.config.php** file:

```php
'list' => array(
  'type'   => 'Segment',
  'options' => array(
    'route'   => '/test/list[/:page]',
    'constraints' => array(
      'page'    => '[0-9]*',
    ),
    'defaults' => array(
      // ...
      'actioncache' => 1,
```

```
      'tags' => array('exam-list')
    ),
  ),
)
```

Finally, we can add the following change to our page and action caching code in the **module/Application/Module.php** file:

```php
public function saveActionCache(MvcEvent $event)
{
        $match = $event->getRouteMatch();
        if(!$match) {
                return;
        }

        if($match->getParam('actioncache')) {
          //..
          if($result instanceof ViewModel) {
            $cache = $event->getApplication()->getServiceManager()->get('cache');
            //..
            $cache->setItem($cacheKey, $content);
            $tags = $match->getParam('tags');
            if($tags) {
                $cache->setTags($cacheKey, $tags);
            }
          }
        }
    }

// ..

public function savePageCache(MvcEvent $event)
{
    $match = $event->getRouteMatch();
    if(!$match) {
        return;
    }

    if($match->getParam('pagecache')) {
        // ...
        $cache->setItem($cacheKey, $data);
        $tags = $match->getParam('tags');
        if($tags) {
                $cache->setTags($cacheKey, $tags);
        }
    }
}
}
```

If you want to get the source code, run these commands:

```
cd <full/path/to/>/learnzf2/
git stash
git checkout 'ch-cache'
```

Better Development Productivity

To increase your productivity you can use tools that help you write and debug code, find problems, and also speed up code execution. In this chapter I will show how *Zend Studio* and *Zend Server* can be used in combination, or separately, to help you to develop better ZF2 applications.

> **Disclaimer**
> I work for Zend, but I am also fan of both their free and paid products. You can develop ZF2 applications without using Zend's products, but with them development is much faster, streamlined, and less error prone. It is up to you to decide if you should use them. Remember that some of the features that these product have are completely free.

Zend Studio

Zend Studio is an IDE (Integrated Development Environment) for PHP developers that can help you to write ZF2 code faster, maintain and organize your code more efficiently, and solve problems more quickly. You can download Zend Studio from the *zend.com* website. After installation you can use all features for a limited period of time, after which only some of the features will be available for free.

The three major features that we will use are:

- remote debug
- code assistance
- wizards

The remote debug feature is available in the free version whereas ZF2 code assistance and wizards are available only in the paid version.

Code (or content) assistance lets you immediately understand which methods or variables are currently in scope, what is their syntax, where are they defined, and what are they doing. The wizards allow you to easily easily new ZF2 modules, controllers and view helpers. The *zend.com* website contains videos[44] that demonstrate these features. When using namespaced classes in your code, Zend Studio will give you a list of classes that match the required class, and will automatically add the correct "use" statement for you.

Zend Server

Zend Server is a PHP application server that can be used to improve application performance and security, as well as to facilitate development. Zend Server comes in different versions, suitable for a wide range of target groups: from a single beginning PHP developer to a multinational company that has a large cluster of PHP servers.

You can download the latest Zend Server version from the *zend.com* website and install it on your server. At the time of this writing you get up to a month of free usage for all features. After the trial period, only some features will be available if you do not buy a license. Debugging is part of the free feature set, and can help you understand the operation of your code and to spot problems. Other components, such as *Monitoring* and *Code Tracing*, help to monitor and analyze the real-time performance of your PHP application, but require a valid license once the month long trial period has expired.

---

44 http://static.zend.com/topics/studio-10/studio10-zf2-video-window.html

Zend Debugger

During the development of this book the Zend Debugger was my best friend, allowing me to gain a better understanding of the inner workings of our ZF2 application. Using the debugger can save you days or even weeks in discovering a problem. In order to use it you need Zend Studio on your development computer, and Zend Server on the machine where the Apache server is running (could be the same machine). In order for the debugger to work flawlessly you need a direct connection between the server and your local machine. For more convenience I installed in Firefox the Zend Studio plugin[45] that will help me launch the debugger directly from the web page giving me problems.

In order to debug a page you have to open it in the browser and then click on the debug button as shown below:

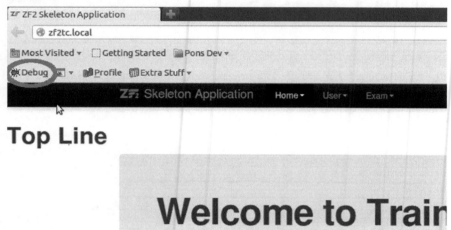

At that moment Zend Studio will open a debug session.

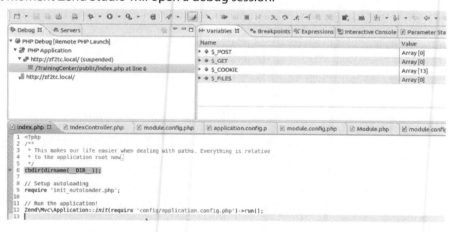

You will be able to see the current source code, taken from the remote server or directly from your project depending on your configuration. You can see the current variables, their values and even change them as you debug.

---

45   http://www.zend.com/en/products/studio/downloads?src=downloadb

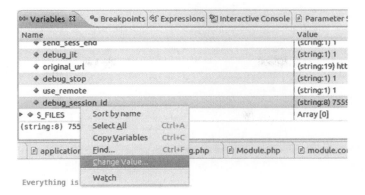

From the toolbar shown below you can navigate through your debug session:

You can go inside of a function or method, jump out of it, or just move to the next line. After every line you will get fresh information about the state of your application and very good idea about the inner workings of the application.

This is how I found a lot more about ZF2 than was indicated in the documentation. You can thus use this for a free boost to your development.

Zend Profiler

Zend Profiler will give you detailed statistical information about the executed code: the number of called files, classes and methods, execution flow, execution time needed and so on. As with Zend Debuger, Zend Profiler needs a direct connection between the server and your local machine to work flawlessly.

In order to activate the profiler you need to press the *Profile* button in the Firefox toolbar.

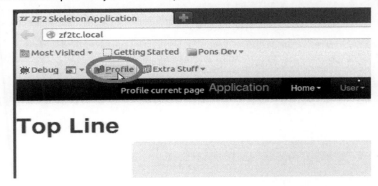

In Zend Studio you will get detailed information similar to this:

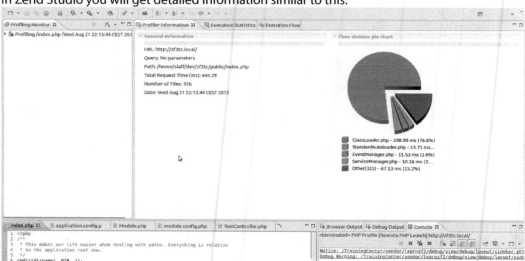

Zend Monitoring

Zend Monitoring is a component that is available only in the paid versions of Zend Server. It can report possible problems in your PHP application, and can also help you to figure out how well your ZF2 application is performing on the current server.

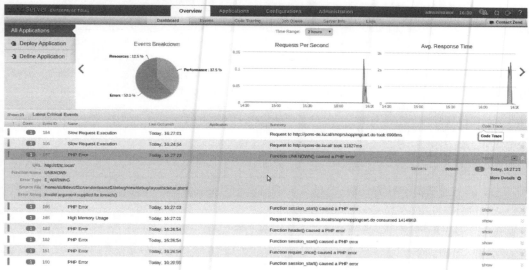

When an event occurs, for example a database error, the person responsible for the database or the PHP code can be informed and act immediately to analyze the problem. Zend Monitor is a must-have if you plan to put your enterprise ZF2 application on a production server and expect to host a lot of visitors.

Zend Code Tracing

Zend Code Tracing is another paid component in Zend Server that helps you discover difficult-to-track problems. It is similar to Zend Profiler but in contrast, information is gathered at the moment the event occurred.

Let's take a look an example. Your ZF2 application is running great, but some hours ago its performance was terrible. With the help of code tracing you can see all function calls, their time and memory consumption, input parameters and return values. You might see, for example, that the credit card processor system was not responding, or that its response was extremely slow. In this manner you would have identified the root cause of the performance problem. You can think of Code Tracing as like a flight recorder: it records information at the time of the problem, allowing you to reconstruct the sequence of events which led to the root problem.

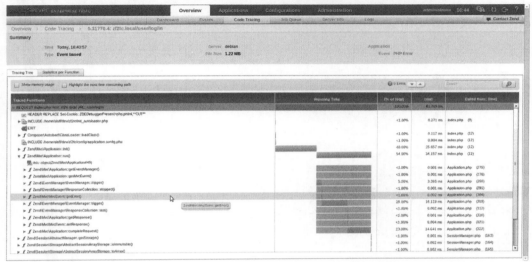

You can read more from the official page[46] on the *zend.com* website.

---

46 http://www.zend.com/en/products/server/zend-server-code-tracing

Award Certificate

For those that took the exams without making a mistake, we can generate a nice award certificate, and send it to them so that they can show it to their friends and colleagues.

PDF Generation

For certificate generation we will use the PDF (Portable Document Format) add-on component from ZF2. In order to install it we need to change the application requirements in the **composer.json** file:

```
"require": {
    "php": ">=5.3.3",
    "zendframework/zendframework": "2.*",
    "doctrine/common": ">=2.1",
    "doctrine/orm": ">=2.1",
    "zendframework/zendpdf": "2.*"
},
"require-dev": {
        „phpunit/phpunit" : „3.7.*"
}
}
```

After that we need to run update:

```
php composer.phar update
```

When someone takes the test and correctly answers 100% of the questions, we can trigger an event. In the Exam module's **Module.php** file we can add a listener to this event which generates a PDF certificate. Because we should keep the *onBootstrap* method as thin as possible, we will use a PDF service to do the work.

```
public function onBootstrap(MvcEvent $event)
{
        $services        = $event->getApplication()->getServiceManager();
        $sharedEventManager = $event->getApplication()
                ->getEventManager()
                ->getSharedManager();
        $sharedEventManager->attach('exam','taken-excellent',
                function($event) use ($services) {
                        $user = $event->getParam('user');
                        $exam = $event->getParam('exam');

                        $pdf = $services->get('pdf');

                        $pdfDocument = $pdf->generateCertificate($user, $exam['name']);
                        //...
                });
}
```

The PDF service code will be saved as **module/Exam/src/Exam/Service/Invokable/Pdf.php** and will have the following initial content:

```php
<?php
namespace Exam\Service\Invokable;

use Zend\ServiceManager\ServiceLocatorAwareInterface;
use Zend\ServiceManager\ServiceLocatorInterface;

use ZendPdf as Pdf;

class Pdf implements ServiceLocatorAwareInterface
{
    /**
     *
     * @var \Zend\ServiceManager\ServiceManager
     */
    protected $services;

    /**
     * Generates certificate of exellence and
     * triggers an event when the file is generated
     * @param \User\Model\Entity\User $user
     * @param \Exam\Model\Test $exam
     */
    public function generateCertificate($user, $exam)
    {
        $config = $this->services->get('config');
        //@todo: Create the Award Certificate PDF
    }

    /* (non-PHPdoc)
     * @see \Zend\ServiceManager\ServiceLocatorAwareInterface::setServiceLocator()
     */
    public function setServiceLocator(ServiceLocatorInterface $serviceLocator) {
            $this->services = $serviceLocator;
    }

    /* (non-PHPdoc)
     * @see \Zend\ServiceManager\ServiceLocatorAwareInterface::getServiceLocator()
     */
```

The highlighted lines contain the code that will generate the PDF.

To generate a PDF document we need to create an instance of ZendPdf\PdfDocument.

```php
<?php
use ZendPdf\PdfDocument;
```

```
$pdf = new PdfDocument();
```

Once we have the PdfDocument instance we need to add pages to it:

```
'$pdf = new PdfDocument();
$page = $pdf->newPage(PdfPage::SIZE_A4)
$pdf->pages[] = $page;
```

The *pages* attribute is an array that contains all the pages in the document. Once we have a page we can draw some shapes or write some text on it.

Before writing text we must set a font. You can use one of the default fonts and define them by name. Below we get the *times bold* font:

```
$font = PdfFont::fontWithName(PdfFont::FONT_TIMES_BOLD);
$page->setFont($font, 40);
$page->drawText($examName, 200, 120);
```

Let's put everything together in a *generateCertificate* method. We will also create a *certificateAction* method in the **Test** controller which will be used to render our PDF:

```
/**
 * Generates award certificate
 * @param \User\Model\Entity\User $user
 * @param string $examName
 */
public function generateCertificate($user, $examName)
{
        $pdf = new PdfDocument();
        $pdf->pages[] = ($page = $pdf->newPage(PdfPage::SIZE_A4));
        $font = PdfFont::fontWithName(PdfFont::FONT_TIMES_BOLD);
        $page->setFont($font, 40);
        $page->drawText($examName, 200, 120);

        return $pdf;
}
```

The *certificateAction* can look like this:

```
public function certificateAction()
{
        $pdfService = $this->serviceLocator->get('pdf');
        $user = $this->serviceLocator->get('user');
        $user->setName('John Smith');
        $pdf = $pdfService->generateCertificate($user, "Exam Name");

        $response = $this->getResponse();

        // We need to set a content-type header so that the
```

```
// browser is able to recognize our pdf and display it
$response->getHeaders()
                    ->addHeaderLine('Content-Type: application/pdf');


$response->setContent($pdf->render());

// if we want to shortcut the execution we just return the
// response object and then the view and the layout are not
// rendered at all
return $response;
}
```

Don't forget to change the ACL for the Exam module, allowing access to users with the "admin" role. If you don't have a user with an "admin" role, be sure to add one, and to log his email and password.

In the web browser navigate to the URL **/exam/test/certificate.** You may be a bit disappointed. Let's face it – at the moment the award certificate is quite ugly! The PDF component works only with basic operations such as adding text, setting fonts, drawing shapes, setting colors, and so forth. Nevertheless it has one killer feature: it can import an existing PDF document, using it as a template. That is exactly what we are planning to do for our PDF service. We will read the local path to the template file stored in the config under the key *pdf –> exam_certificate*. Let's add this definition to our Exam module configuration:

```
'pdf' => array(
            'exam_certificate' => __DIR__.'/../samples/pdf/exam_certificate.pdf',
        )
```

We will then change the *generateCertificate* method so that it looks like this:

```
public function generateCertificate($user, $examName)
{
        $config = $this->services->get('config');
        $pdf = PdfDocument::load($config['pdf']['exam_certificate']);

        $page = $pdf->pages[0];
        $font = PdfFont::fontWithName(PdfFont::FONT_TIMES_BOLD);
        $page->setFont($font, 40);
        $page->drawText($examName, 200, 120);

        return $pdf;
}
```

Although this looks better now, we can do more with ZendPdf. ZendPdf allows us to use the nice fonts come with this document. If you want to see their names and standard text, you can extract them:

226 LEARN ZEND FRAMEWORK 2

```php
public function generateCertificate($user, $examName)
{
        $config = $this->services->get('config');
        $pdf = PdfDocument::load($config['pdf']['exam_certificate']);

        $page = $pdf->pages[0];

        $font = PdfFont::fontWithName(PdfFont::FONT_TIMES_BOLD);
        $page->setFont($font, 40);
        $page->drawText($examName, 200, 120);

        $fontList = $pdf->extractFonts();

        $yPosition = 600;
        foreach ($fontList as $font) {
                $page->setFont($font, 15);
                $fontName = $font->getFontName(PdfFont::NAME_POSTSCRIPT,
                                'en',
                                'UTF-8');
                $page->drawText($fontName.': The quick brown fox jumps over the lazy dog',
                                100,
                                $yPosition,
                                'UTF-8');
                $yPosition -= 30;
        }

        return $pdf;
```

If we refresh the browser page we will see that the pdf document has content similar to the image shown below:

We will use the nice AdineKirnberg-Script font and the new version of our certificate generation now looks like this:

```php
public function generateCertificate($user, $examName)
{
        $config = $this->services->get('config');
        $pdf = PdfDocument::load($config['pdf']['exam_certificate']);

        // get the first page
        $page = $pdf->pages[0];

        // Extract the AdineKirnberg-Script font included in the PDF sample
        $font = $page->extractFont(,AdineKirnberg-Script');
        $page->setFont($font, 80);

        // and write the name of the user with it
        $page->drawText($user->getName(), 200, 280);

        // after that use Time Bold to write the name of the exam
        $font = PdfFont::fontWithName(PdfFont::FONT_TIMES_BOLD);
        $page->setFont($font, 40);
        $page->drawText($examName, 200, 120);

        return $pdf;
}
```

Finally, we may want to add the ZF2 icon to the certificate. This can be done using the following code:

```php
public function generateCertificate($user, $examName)
{
        $config = $this->services->get('config');
        // ...
        // after that use Time Bold to write the name of the exam
        $font = PdfFont::fontWithName(PdfFont::FONT_TIMES_BOLD);
        $page->setFont($font, 40);
        $page->drawText($examName, 200, 120);

        // We use the png image from the public/images folder
        $imageFile = 'public/images/zf2-logo.png';
        // get the right size to do some calculations
        $size = getimagesize($imageFile);
        // load the image
        $image = \ZendPdf\Image::imageWithPath($imageFile);
        $x = 580;
        $y = 440;
        // and finally draw the image
        $page->drawImage($image, $x, $y, $x+$size[0], $y+$size[1]);

        return $pdf;
}
```

At this point, our improved sample award certificate should appear as shown below:

We are almost at the end of our PDF generation saga. This means we can start the new topic – sending email. To bind them together we will have the *onBootstrap* method trigger a new event once the PDF is generated. The code can look like this:

```
public function onBootstrap(MvcEvent $event)
{
    $services = $event->getApplication()->getServiceManager();
    $sharedEventManager = $event->getApplication()
            ->getEventManager()
            ->getSharedManager();

    $sharedEventManager->attach('exam','taken-excellent',
            function($event) use ($services) {
    $user = $event->getParam('user');
    $exam = $event->getParam('exam');

    $pdf = $services->get('pdf');
    $pdfDocument = $pdf->generateCertificate($user, $exam['name']);

    $newEvent = new EventManager('exam');
    $newEvent->trigger('certificate-generated', $this, array (
            'user' => $event->getParam('user'),
            'exam' => $event->getParam('exam'),
            'pdf' => $pdfDocument
    ));
    });
}
```

What the highlighted lines do is to send the event **certificate-generated** on the channel **exam** and pass as a parameter the user, exam information and PDF document.

If you want to get the source code, type these commands:

```
cd <full/path/to/>/learnzf2/
git stash
git checkout 'ch-pdf'
```

Mail

The time has come to mail our PDF file to the genuis that finished the test with such great success. For that purpose we will use the Zend\Mail component. One of its key features, among others, is that it allows us to include attachments.

The minum requirement to send email with Zend\Mail is to have at least one *recepient* and one message *body*. The sample code below shows this and also sets the *subject* and *from* fields:

```
use Zend\Mail;

$mail = new Mail\Message();
```

```
$mail->setBody('You are genius! You answered all the questions correctly.
Therefore, in appreciation, we are sending this free award certificate.');
$mail->setFrom('sender@example.org', 'Sender\'s name');
$mail->addTo('user@email', 'User name');
$mail->setSubject('Congratulations: Here is your award certificate');
```

Now in order to send our email we must specify a *transport*. The following lines send the email via *sendmail:*

```
'cache-enabled-services' => array(
        'translator',
    ),
```

Let's put that information in a new service called *mail* that will do the work for us. We will save the service in **module/ Exam/src/Exam/Service/Invokable/Mail.php**.

The initial code of our service is the following:

```php
<?php
namespace Exam\Service\Invokable;

use Zend\ServiceManager\ServiceLocatorAwareInterface;
use Zend\ServiceManager\ServiceLocatorInterface;
use Zend\Mail\Message;

class Mail implements ServiceLocatorAwareInterface
{
        /**
         *
         * @var \Zend\ServiceManager\ServiceManager
         */
        protected $services;

        /**
         * Sends award certificate
         *
         * @param \User\Model\Entity\User $user
         * @param array $exam
         * @param \ZendPdf\Document $pdf
         */
        public function sendCertificate($user, $exam, $pdf)
        {
                $translateService = $this->services->get('translate');
                $mail = new Message();
                $mail->addTo($user->getEmail(), $user->getName());

$text = 'You are a genius!
You answered all the questions correctly.
```

Therefore, in appreciation, we are sending you this free award certificate.

```
';
                $mail->setBody($text);
                $mail->setFrom('slaff@linux-bg.org', 'Slavey Karadzhov');
                $mail->setSubject($translateService->translate(
        'Congratulations: Here is your award certificate'));
                // todo ...
        }

        /* (non-PHPdoc)
         * @see \Zend\ServiceManager\ServiceLocatorAwareInterface::setServiceLocator()
         */
        public function setServiceLocator(ServiceLocatorInterface $serviceLocator) {
                $this->services = $serviceLocator;
        }

        /* (non-PHPdoc)
         * @see \Zend\ServiceManager\ServiceLocatorAwareInterface::getServiceLocator()
         */
        public function getServiceLocator() {
                return $this->services;
        }
}
```

Don't forget to register the service in the Exam module configuration.

```
'service_manager'=> array (
    'invokables' => array(
        // ...
        'pdf'       => 'Exam\Service\Invokable\Pdf',
        'mail'      => 'Exam\Service\Invokable\Mail',
    )
),
```

In order to attach an item to the email we have to create *parts*. Please note that when using parts, the original body needs to be given as a part.

```
<?php
namespace Exam\Service\Invokable;

use Zend\ServiceManager\ServiceLocatorAwareInterface;
use Zend\ServiceManager\ServiceLocatorInterface;
use Zend\Mail\Message;
use Zend\Mime\Message as MimeMessage;
use Zend\Mime\Part as MimePart;

class Mail implements ServiceLocatorAwareInterface
```

```php
{
        // ..
        public function sendCertificate($user, $exam, $pdf)
        {
                $translator = $this->services->get('translator');
                $mail = new Message();
                $mail->addTo($user->getEmail(), $user->getName());

$text = 'You are a genius!
You answered all the questions correctly.
Therefore, in appreciation, we are sending you this free award certificate.

';
                // we create a new mime message
                $mimeMessage = new MimeMessage();
                // create the original body as part
                $textPart = new MimePart($text);
                $textPart->type = "text/plain";
                // add the pdf document as a second part
                $pdfPart = new MimePart($pdf->render());
                $pdfPart->type = 'application/pdf';
                $mimeMessage->setParts(array($textPart, $pdfPart));

                $mail->setBody($mimeMessage);

                $mail->setFrom('slaff@linux-bg.org', 'Slavey Karadzhov');
                $mail->setSubject($translator->translate('Congratulations: Here is your
award certificate'));

                $transport = $this->services->get('mail-transport');
                $transport->send($mail);
        }
        // ...
}
```

The mail is actually sent by the mail transport. In our code above the mail transport represents another service that we can use, and override, if needed.

At the moment of this writing Zend\Mail comes with three transports:

- Sendmail
- Smtp
- File

The File transport is useful for testing purposes, and this is the one that we will use for now. Let's create the new *mail-transport* service. It will reside in **module/Exam/src/Exam/Service/Factory/MailTransport.php**

```php
<?php
namespace Exam\Service\Factory;
```

```php
use Zend\ServiceManager\FactoryInterface;
use Zend\ServiceManager\ServiceLocatorInterface;
use Zend\Mail\Transport\File as FileTransport;
use Zend\Mail\Transport\FileOptions;

class MailTransport implements FactoryInterface
{
        /* (non-PHPdoc)
         * @see \Zend\ServiceManager\FactoryInterface::createService()
         */
        public function createService(ServiceLocatorInterface $serviceLocator)
        {
                $transport = new FileTransport();
                $options  = new FileOptions(array(
                                'path'          => 'data/mail/',
                                'callback'            => function (FileTransport $transport) {
                                    return 'Message_' . microtime(true) . '_' . mt_rand() . '.txt';
                                },
                ));
                $transport->setOptions($options);

                return $transport;

        }
}
```

Be sure to create a new directory called **mail** under **<full/path/to/>/learnzf2/data/** that is writable by the web server user. Also, don't forget the registration of the service:

```php
'service_manager'=> array (
        'factories' => array(
                'mail-transport' => 'Exam\Service\Factory\MailTransport'
        ),
        'invokables' => array(
//...
)
```

Finally, we need to attach a listener to the *exam/certificate-created* event before the actual triggering of the event. So the final code for the *onBootstrap* method now looks like this:

```php
public function onBootstrap(MvcEvent $event)
{
        $services       = $event->getApplication()->getServiceManager();
        $sharedEventManager = $event->getApplication()
                ->getEventManager()
                ->getSharedManager();

        $sharedEventManager->attach('exam','certificate-generated',
```

```php
                    function($event) use ($services) {
                    $mail = $services->get('mail');
                    $user = $event->getParam('user');
                    $exam = $event->getParam('exam');
                    $pdf  = $event->getParam('pdf');

                    $mail->sendCertificate($user, $exam, $pdf);
        });

        $sharedEventManager->attach('exam','taken-excellent',
                function($event) use ($services) {
                        $user = $event->getParam('user');
                        $exam = $event->getParam('exam');

                        $pdf = $services->get('pdf');
                        $pdfDocument = $pdf->generateCertificate($user, $exam['name']);

                        $newEvent = new EventManager('exam');
                        $newEvent->trigger('certificate-generated', $this, array (
                                        'user' => $event->getParam('user'),
                                        'exam' => $event->getParam('exam'),
                                        'pdf'  => $pdfDocument
        ));
    });
}
```

If you want to get the source code, type these commands:

```
cd <full/path/to/>/learnzf2/
git stash
git checkout 'ch-mail'
```

Better Package Management

We are almost finished with our application and its modules. The sections below describe how to prepare for the final steps: packaging, managing and distribution of the modules.

Understanding Composer

What we have created are 3 reusable modules that can help to build other projects. In order to use and distribute them we need appropriate tools. *Composer* is one such tool. It allows us to create and to distribute packages from our source code. What we will do now is to create distributable packages out of our modules. We will demonstrate how to do this for only one of the modules. You would just need to repeat these steps to do the same for the other two modules.

Creating a Package

To create a package from your module you will need to add a **composer.json** file that describes its content. As the name suggests, it has to be a valid JSON file and needs to contain certain fields. According to the composer documentation[47] the two required fields for packages are *name* and *description*. We will add also *authors* to identify the current authors of the module. The **composer.json** file could look like this:

```
{
        "name": "learnzf2/debug",
        "description": "Debug module from the \"Learn ZF2\" book",
        "authors": [
                {
                    "name": "Slavey Karadzhov",
                    "email": "slaff@linux-bg.org",
                    "homepage": "http://zf2consulting.com",
                    "role": "Author"
                },
        ]
}
```

This is the minimum set of requirements for describing our first package, which can now be submitted to our version control system (VCS).

Describing Dependencies

Our Exam package depends on the User package. In composer this can be defined using the "require" field. The definition of the **module/Exam/composer.json** file is as follows:

```
{
        "name": "learnzf2/exam",
        "description": "Exam module from the \"Learn ZF2\" book",
        "authors": [
                {
                    "name": "Slavey Karadzhov",
```

```
            "email": "slaff@linux-bg.org",
            "homepage": "http://www.linux-bg.de",
            "role": "Author"
        },
    ],

    'require': {
            "learnzf2/user": "dev-master"
    }
}
```

The line in grey indicates that our Exam package requires the package with:

- vendor prefix **learnzf2**
- name **user**
- version **"dev-master"**

The **"dev-master"** version is a reserved keyword that is used to represent the latest unstable version from the master branch. If you want to specify an exact version instead of "dev-master" you can write a specific version number (i.e. "1.0.2"), or use wildcards for getting the latest numbered version (i.e. "1.0.*").

In the *require* section you can also specify the minimum version of PHP your package needs. Adding the following to the *require* section specifies that the minimum allowed version of PHP is 5.3.3. Version constraints are described in great detail in the composer website[48].

```
    ],
    'require': {
            "learnzf2/user" : "dev-master",
            "php"           : ">=5.3.3",
    }
}
```

In the User module we used Doctrine 2. In the Exam module we used ZendPdf. Also, in the User module, we required Zend Framework 2 and PHPUnit as a *development* requirement. Below is the final definition of the *require* sections for the Debug, User and Exam modules.

Debug module:

```
"require": {
        "php": ">=5.3.3",
        "zendframework/zendframework": "2.*"
},
```

User module:

```
"require": {
        "php": ">=5.3.3",
        "zendframework/zendframework": "2.*",
```

```
        "doctrine/common": ">=2.1",
        "doctrine/orm": ">=2.1"
},
"require-dev": {
        "phpunit/phpunit": "3.7.*"
},
```

And Exam module:

```
"require": {
        "php": ">=5.3.3",
        "zendframework/zendframework": "2.*",
        "learnzf2/user": "dev-master",
        "zendframework/zendpdf": "2.*"
},
```

Autoloader Configuration

As our modules contain source code, we would like to give hints to composer as to where to auto load these files. To achieve this we need to specify the *autoload* key. For the Debug module we need the following:

```
"autoload": {
    "psr-0": {
        "Exam\\": „src/"
    },
    "classmap": [
        "Module.php"
    ]
}
```

The *psr-0* key specifies that all classes starting with Exam namespace can be found under the **src/** sub-directory (the **src/** directory is relative to the location of the **composer.json** file.) The *classmap* key instructs the autoloader to include the **Module.php** file when autoloading classes with the Exam namespace.

Publishing Packages

Separating the Source Code

In order to use and publish the modules in public or private repositories, we need to create a separate git repository for each module. I will use *github.com* and below will show you how to put one of the modules into a separate repository. Separating the other modules is a similar procedure.

1. Create a new repository on *github.com*. I will name it **learnzf2-debug**
2. Commit the existing module code to the repository. This can be achieved with the following commands:

```
cd module/Debug
git init
git add *
git commit -m "Initial version of separate ,LearnZF2 Debug' module"
git remote add origin https://github.com/<your-user>/learnzf-debug.git
git push -u origin master
```

The source code for the Debug module is now uploaded to my new github repository. You can see it from this URL: https://github.com/slaff/learnzf-debug. This was just preparation for the next step: creating a package out of our separated module code.

Public Repositories

Composer has a default public repository where you can publish all your packages, allowing anybody to use them. The name of the repository where you can publish your packages is **packagist.org**. At the moment the procedure is pretty straight forward. You just need to specify the public VCS URL and follow the wizard.

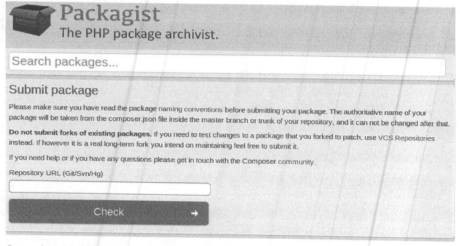

Screenshot: 1 Publishing packages to Packigist.org

In my case I need to enter https://github.com/slaff/learnzf-debug.git and follow the instructions. Once I am done, I can completely remove the **module/Debug** directory and add to the **composer.json** file, located in the main application directory, the following requirement:

```
"require": {
    "php": ">=5.3.3",
    "zendframework/zendframework": "2.*",
    //...
    "learnzf2/debug": "dev-master"
},
```

I can now fetch the module by running the following command:

```
php composer.phar update
```

Our Debug module will appear under **vendor/learnzf2/debug/**.

Private Repositories

Composer can also use other repositories. For your company you may define a private repository that gets its data from different locations. The composer page has an article[49] about this.

As an example, suppose we wish to use a private *git* repository as source for our data. In a completely new project we can create a **composer.json** file that has the following definition:

```
"repositories": [
  {
    "type": "vcs",
    "url": "git@bitbucket.org/slaff/learnzf2-debug"
  }
],
"require": {
  "php": ">=5.3.3",
  "zendframework/zendframework": "2.*",
  "learnzf2/debug": "dev-master"
}
}
```

Assuming you have access to this repository, you could run this command:

```
php composer.phar update
```

Composer will retrieve the master branch from the private *git* repository and will look for a **composer.json** file in the main directory. According to the one we added just now, it would figure out that in this repository there is a **learnzf2/debug** package. At that point the required packages would then be installed.

The parameter *type "vcs"* tells Composer to try to determine automatically what type of VCS you have. At the time of this writing the supported VCS are *git*, *subversion* and *mercurial*. You can use type values "git", "svn" or "hg" instead of "vcs" to specify explicitly what type of VCS you have.

To check for updates just run:

```
php composer.phar update
```

Replacing Packages

Let's say you cloned our *learnzf2/user* model and made substantial improvements. If you want to use this module instead of the original, and want to use a new package name for it, in the definition of your improved module you must add a **replace** definition. Otherwise, packages that require the original, like *learnzf2/exam* for example, will complain about unmet dependencies.

Your new **composer.json** should look like this:

```
{
        "name": "my-vendor-previx/user",
        "description": "Improved user module from the \"Learn ZF2\" book",
        "authors": [
```

```
        {
            "name": "John Smith",
            "email": "name@subdomain.domain",
            "homepage": "http://homepage.url",
            "role": "Contributor"
        },
        {
            "name": "Slavey Karadzhov",
            "email": "slaff@linux-bg.org",
            "homepage": "http://www.linux-bg.de",
            "role": "Author"
        }
    ],
    "replace": {
        "zf2book/user": "self.version"
    }
}
```

The definition above says that your new package replaces the *learnzf2/user* package and it replaces the same version as the one that *learnzf2* was providing. If this is not the case then next to the *version* key you should specify the version(s) that are replaced.

Scripts

Additional actions that have to be performed during installation or update of a package can be automated with Composer. This can be achieved using composer scripts.

"A script, in Composer's terms, can either be a PHP callback (defined as a static method) or any command-line executable command. Scripts are useful for executing a package's custom code or package-specific commands during the Composer execution process." [50].

There are different phases during which you can execute scripts. Composer fires the following named events during its execution process:

Event	Occurs ...
pre-install-cmd	before the install command is executed
post-install-cmd	after the install command is executed
pre-update-cmd	before the update command is executed
post-update-cmd	after the update command is executed
pre-package-install	before a package is installed
post-package-install	after a package is installed
pre-package-update	before a package is updated
post-package-update	after a package is updated
pre-package-uninstall	before a package has been uninstalled
post-package-uninstall	after a package has been uninstalled

---

50 http://getcomposer.org/doc/articles/scripts.md

post-autoload-dump	after the autoloader is dumped, either during install/up-date, or via the dump-autoload command

For example, our User module provides a **database.local.php.dist** configuration. Instead of manually copying this file to the application config directory, we can add the following lines to our **module/User/composer.json** file:

```
"scripts": {
        "post-package-install": [
                "cp config/database.local.php.dist ../../config/autoload/database.local.php"
        ],
}
```

Composer also allows you to use PHP scripts to execute additional actions. Be sure to read the Composer documentation for examples.

Making Changes to Package and Application

If you want to develop your application and a separate module at the same time, you should commit the application changes as before. For the package, however, first enter the directory where the package was downloaded. For the Debug module that was **vendor/learnzf2/de-bug**. It contains the source code and already initialized *git* repository for this specific package. If you make changes to the package you can commit them and then push them to the remote repository. A sample session can look like this:

```
cd vendor/learnzf2/debug
# make thanges to the README.md file...
git add README.md
git commit -m "Changed something..."
git push https://github.com/slaff/learnzf-debug.git master
```

If you want to get the source code, type these commands:

```
cd <full/path/to/>/learnzf2/
git stash
git checkout 'ch-composer'
php composer.phar update # This is important in order to fetch the learnzf2/debug package
```

Final Words

There is a small surprise for you running the following commands:

```
cd <full/path/to/>/learnzf2/
git stash
git checkout 'ch-final-words'
```

Login with a user that has the *admin* role. If you do not have one, change your current user role in the database to *admin*. Be sure to log out and then log in again for the changes to take effect. Once logged-in, go to **Exam -> Reset**. In the *exam list* page you should see two new tests that you can take related to namespaces and ZF2. Take the sample exams and enjoy! All the questions from the ZF2 test can be answered if you have carefully read the contents of this book. If some answers are not clear to you, be sure to read the respective chapters again.

The application development in this book will stop here. Although not exhaustively comprehensive, it nonetheless covers a good range of topics that you will need sooner or later in your ZF2 projects. I know that there were a number of very important topics that I did not mention, but I wanted to write a book that gives you a good start, leaving room for you to expand your ZF2 knowledge. From here you can start creating your own applications or continue extending the application presented in the book. Zend Technologies is offering *ZF2 Fundamentals* and *ZF2 Advanced* training courses[51] that you can use to fortify your knowledge and get a real ZF2 certificate.

I hope you have learned a lot and had fun coding, as much as my team and I had creating this book! Your valuable feedback will help us improve this book and the source code. Please write us at <slaff@linux-bg.org> and visit our website at http://learnzf2.com for updates.

---

51 http://www.zend.com/en/services/training/course-catalog/zend-framework-2

ABOUT THE AUTHOR

Slavey Karadzhov is a full time senior consultant at Zend Technologies. He is located in Stuttgart, Germany and travels the world while trying, among other things, to help people get better understanding about programing and Zend Framework in particular.

In his daily work he tackles the problems that developers often face when confronted with Zend Framework 2. Some of the examples in this book are modified versions of real world examples. The solutions provided are among the best possible, backed with years of experience and academical background.

Slavey Karadzhov has two major degrees: one in Software Technology from the University of Applied Science in Stuttgart, Germany, and the other in Computer Science from Sofia University, Bulgaria.

Printed in Great Britain
by Amazon.co.uk, Ltd.,
Marston Gate.